ESCAPING THE ASSEMBLY LINE

*The tools to notice
(and power to change)
the discipleship defaults
that are killing your faith*

Justin Rossow

ESCAPING THE ASSEMBLY LINE:
THE TOOLS TO NOTICE (AND POWER TO CHANGE)
THE DISCIPLESHIP DEFAULTS THAT ARE KILLING YOUR FAITH

BY JUSTIN ROSSOW

© 2025 Justin Rossow and Next Step Press
Imprint: Next Step Press

Scripture quotations marked (ESV) are taken from The Holy Bible, English Standard Version® copyright © 2001 by Crossway, a publishing ministry of Good News Publishers. Used by permission. All rights reserved.

Scripture quotations marked (NIV) are taken from The Holy Bible, New International Version® copyright © 1973, 1978, 1984, 2011 by Biblica, Inc.™ Used by permission of Zondervan. All rights reserved worldwide. www.zondervan.com The "NIV" and "New International Version" are trademarks registered in the United States Patent and Trademark Office by Biblica, Inc.™

Scripture quotations without attribution are the author's own translation.

Internal artwork: Lucie Orozco
Proofreading: Steve Rohrbach, Deanna Rossow, and "Rev" Francis Rossow
Cover design: Brett Jordan, bit.ly/brett_blog
Cover image: Building Aircraft: Making the Engine –
C.R.W. Nevinson, via: unsplash.com/@clevelandart

Inquiries or comments may be directed to Innovation@findmynextstep.org.

Hardcover ISBN: 979-8-9922105-0-7
Paperback ISBN: 979-8-9922105-1-4
Kindle Edition ISBN: 979-8-9922105-2-1

Library of Congress Control Number: 2024926519

We help you take a next step

Praise for *Escaping the Assembly Line*

Finally, a book about discipleship that doesn't make the Christian life sound like homework! Rossow's approach to this often-burdensome subject is **practical yet playful,** abounding in creativity yet grounded in the Good News from start to finish.

With a rare ear for language—and the help of some inspired images—he invites us to interrogate our assumptions about what it means to follow Jesus in ways that are both **unexpected and deeply refreshing.** Watch out: if you're not careful, this book may reignite your excitement about being a Christian.

David Zahl,
author of *Low Anthropology* and *Seculosity*

The first time I heard the ideas in this book I had the rare and delightful feeling of **simultaneously having the rug pulled out from under my feet and landing on home ground for the very first time.** This book will shake you up so that you find things settling in better places than they were before.

Pretend you've been pedaling a racing bike around the town for a year and one day some guy shows you how to change gears. The bike is your Christian life, and that guy is Justin Rossow.

Dr. Conrad Gempf,
author of *Jesus Asked* and *Mealtime Habits of the Messiah*

Rossow uncovers the confusions and misconceptions we have unknowingly adopted as defaults in the church, often accidentally missing the heart of Jesus at the same time. Gently inviting a wider approach, **Rossow offers hope and grace for walking with God and others in our daily lives.** His accessible creativity makes shifting your perspective a joy as you grow in faith and discipleship.

Dcs. Heidi Goehmann, LCSW, LMSW,
author of *Finding Hope* and *Emotions & the Gospel*

I love this book! **I wish I'd read something like this when I was burning out in my parish,** feeling like I was working for a factory, and having a hard time convincing people that we could follow Jesus in a more organic way.

Escaping the Assembly Line offers something I couldn't find in those years: a way to *rethink how we think*; different ways to conceptualize habits that seem so obvious, but keep us stuck. My prayer is that people read this book and understand it for what it is: **a friendly challenge, with insights that actually help.**

Dr. Alexandre Vieira
Assistant Professor of Exegetical Theology,
Concordia Lutheran Seminary, Alberta, CA

For years, I felt something was amiss. I couldn't pinpoint what it was and lacked the vocabulary or concepts to articulate the missing piece. I simply knew that **our discussions about faith and faith formation were incomplete. There were too many underlying assumptions.** Justin's words and thought process helped me shed these assumptions. Don't worry, he doesn't throw the baby out with the bathwater; but he will **help you develop the eyes to see** the water you are swimming in.

Rev. Ben Gonzales,
District Discipleship Development and
Mission Strategist, Texas District, LCMS

As a teacher and preacher of the Gospel, **I could not put this book down!** Justin gives us eyes to see how we envision discipleship and mission in problematic ways so that the Holy Spirit can reshape our vision in and through the Word of God. The metaphors and images are concrete, drawn from Scripture and real experience. **Here is a book you will use.**

Rev. Theodore J. Hopkins, Ph.D.
Senior Pastor, St. Paul, Ann Arbor and author of
Christ, Church, and World and (with Robert Kolb) *The Christian Faith*

For my Great Uncle, Professor "Rev" Francis Rossow,
who wrote *Preaching the Creative Gospel Creatively*
and spent a career doing the same.

Celebrating his 100th birthday.

Contents

Introduction: Longing for Something More..1

1. Assembly Line or Adventure?
   Something More than "Making Disciples"...13

2. Fish Discover Water Last: Rethinking How We Think..........................31

3. High Bar or Clay Jar?
   Something More than "Trying to be like Jesus"......................................44

4. Relay Race or Rope Team?
   Something More than "Passing on the Faith"...69

5. What You See is What You Get:
   The Wisdom of Changing Your Lenses...89

6. Bank Vault or Banquet?
   Something More than "Outreach"...107

7. Pitched Battle or Pitched Tent?
   Something More than "Defending the Truth".....................................137

Conclusion: GPA or GPS? Where do we go from here? 164

Acknowledgements...179
Works Cited..180
Index of Metaphors..183
Index of Scripture References..187
More from Next Step Press 189

Resource Page

For bonus material, expanded conversation, and other related content visit **https://bit.ly/etal-Resource.** You'll find:

- The original From Assembly Line to Adventure sermon from a conference for pastors in Fort Worth, Texas.

- A Prezi that combines content from chapters 6 and 7.

- A sermon where people actually run the relay race in chapter 4.

- Other links, podcast episodes, and resources to enhance your read.

We hope to see you there!

Introduction

Longing for Something More

If you share even a vague sense that *something in the Church just is not working right*, then this book is for you...

I was talking to a friend about "discipleship" recently. She had some honest questions about my use of the word. For her, "discipleship" has always been a church gimmick, a one-size-fits-all cookie-cutter approach that ensures "success" by following a set formula. In her experience, people who push "discipleship programs" want you to use their four-step, magic bullet method, and then keep track of how many disciples you have "made."

Tracking results (my friend called it "counting scalps") helps validate their program. As a participant, you are supposed to feel good about the disciples you have "made." And if you don't have enough "notches on your belt" (her phrase), then there must be something wrong with *you*...

My friend works in the church and is married to a pastor. They have served together at several vibrant, forward-thinking, growing congregations. And the way these churches imagined outreach left their church workers feeling beat up by the process. To my friends, it seems like there must be something more to "discipleship" than a formulaic program we so often use as Law...

This book if for them.

According to ongoing research, the number of people who self-identify as having no religious affiliation keeps going up year to year, making "Nones" the fastest growing "religious group" in America.[1] The Christian Church has always struggled to pass the faith onto the next generation. But young people are leaving and never coming back in numbers we aren't used to seeing.

And COVID didn't help one bit! In many congregations, or even most, membership and attendance continue to decline. The people who remain are left feeling like there must be something more to "following Jesus" than just sitting in a pew for an hour on Sunday. If my faith is so important, why doesn't it make more of a difference during the rest of my week...? This book is for them, too.

---

[1] According to Pew Research, "Nones" may be stabilizing around 28% of the US population as of Jan, 2024, or at least growing more gradually: https://www.pewresearch.org/short-reads/2024/01/24/has-the-rise-of-religious-nones-come-to-an-end-in-the-us/.

Ask any lay person, any pastor, anyone even remotely connected to the idea that Jesus is somehow important to life in the world today, and they likely have a story to share—an anecdote about how their home religious institution just doesn't align with the way they think Church is supposed to be.

We can sense it. We feel the disconnect. We know it, even if we hate to admit it. So this book if for all of us.

Something about our default ways of *being a Christian* or even *being the Church* just isn't working right, leaving longtime believers with a vague sense that there must be more to faith and following Jesus than *this*.

But what? What is that *something more*?

In one sense, the religious institution we experience in the local church has always diverged from the Body of Christ as we imagine it should be. The church around the corner has always fallen short of being what the Church is supposed to be, because every congregation has always been filled with *people* who fall short of who they are supposed to be. And as long as sin endures (which won't be always), local churches will also be sinful, even as the Church is already loved and forgiven and beautiful because of Jesus.

Fine and good. But even taking our fallen, sinful reality into account, **something about the default ways we live out our lives together as sinful-but-forgiven people of God just isn't functioning the way Jesus intends.** The community doesn't act like a community; the Body doesn't function as a body; the one place that should give hope and life and courage feels just as divisive and empty as every other social group or political organization.

Of course, no single church is perfect.

Of course, God still uses the Church to bring faith and hope and restoration.

Of course, we walk by faith and not by sight; and we shouldn't be surprised if the power (or even the effectiveness) of the whole Christian Church on earth is often hidden from our view.

But, doggone it! Something's just not right here! The institution that seemed so vibrant just a generation or two ago no longer feels so *alive*.

It's as if the Church sensed a looming cultural threat, so we stopped dead in our tracks and circled the wagons. It's as if we traded in our sense of *exploration* in order to buy some semblance of *safety*—a stagnant status quo that isn't really "safe" at all. It's as if we tried to *protect* what's most important to us the best way we knew how; but in so doing, lost sight of *what's actually most important*.

The culture has certainly shifted around the Church over the last half-century or so. But the problem is something more than cultural. The default ways we imagine faith and following have gotten us where we are today; and now we sense that **the same ways of thinking just can't get us any farther.**

So it's OK if you find yourself longing for something more. You are not crazy for feeling disoriented or discontented. If you share even a vague sense that something in our Church default settings just isn't working right, then this book is for you. Your struggle is real; don't give up yet. There *is* something more.

But how do we find that *something more?*

I don't think we can solve our *sin* problem until Jesus himself does away with sin, death, and the devil. (Come quickly, Lord!) But I do think we can explore different ways to live out what it means to be Christian individuals or a Christian community, ways that the Spirit can use to breathe new life into our understanding and imagining, our thinking and our living.

The place to begin this renewed reformation is with our basic Christian default settings. **How we think *matters*. Our defaults determine more than we know.** What we naturally *assume* following Jesus is *supposed to* look like—and how we typically *imagine* a community of believers—affects what we think we are doing, the kinds of decision we assume we need to make, and how we go about making those decisions.

We aren't going to "fix" the Church. But **we can notice places where the way we normally talk, feel, imagine, act, and think about *being Church* leads to a distorted experience of following Jesus.** And we can look for *other* ways, other more biblical and more beautiful ways, of thinking about our life of following and our mission in the world—ways that can lead us toward **more faithful talking, feeling, imagining, and acting out** our status as sinful-but-forgiven members of God's eternal family.

Sometimes, the way we have naturally come to envision our life of faith is *kind of* right, *almost* right, right *in a narrow sense*, but with unhelpful and unhealthy unintended consequences. And sometimes, unintentionally and unconsciously, the way we imagine the Church actually undermines or contradicts the Bible's vision of the Church in the world. That's when our natural assumptions do the most damage to our faith.

Ultimately, this book is an attempt to talk about *what we rarely ever talk about*, because it seems so obvious and natural. We don't bother discussing "what goes without saying." We rarely notice our own default settings. And we almost never bother to think critically about our own uncritical thinking.

Even *detecting* our assumptions poses a significant challenge. But once we get the knack for noticing our natural tendencies, we can begin to imagine something more than our standardized imagination currently allows.

What if that feeling of discontent, that *longing for something more*, is already the work of the Spirit preparing our hearts and minds to rethink how we typically think about faith and following?

Longing for something more is a good beginning.

Noticing your automatic assumptions is an important next step.

A new awareness of your natural tendencies can put your foot on the right path, and help you discover more faithful and more fruitful and more joyful ways of following Jesus.

That exploration of discovery begins here in time, as a kind of warm up for the life of the world to come. But the adventure of following Jesus continues into eternity, further up and further in, as we explore the vast landscape of knowing fully, even as we are fully known.

A Look Ahead

The habitual ways we have of talking about being Church, catch phrases like "outreach" or "making disciples" or even "defending the faith," define Christianity in terms which feel so obvious and natural—so *inherently right*—we don't *need* to think about them in any more specific detail. They just *are*.

In other words, **the way we have grown to understand who we are and what we do has become so calcified with automatic assumptions that we are no longer aware those assumptions are even there.**

But those automatic patterns of thinking shape our expectations, feelings, and actions as individual believers and as congregations. And those assumptions will have to grow and change if we are going to find a more effective, more beautiful, and more biblical way of being Church.

We don't just need better answers to our standard questions about making disciples or defending the faith; **we need better questions** about how to live life as a faith community in an increasingly post-Christian culture. It's time to check our default settings and rethink *how we think* about faith and following.

In Chapter 1 (Assembly Line or Adventure?), we will discover that the standard language of "making disciples" isn't as biblical as we always assumed. To complicate things further, the most natural ways we modern Christians have for *making* something *out of* something else elevates a range of assembly line values—like efficiency, speed, standardization, and professionalization—that don't naturally cultivate authentic disciples. We'll try to rethink discipleship as a kind of *walking with* and see if that captures more of what Jesus meant by "discipling the nations" in the first place.

Many of our standard default settings for discipleship align with the values and assumptions of the Assembly Line. So Chapter 1 sets the stage for the rest of the book as we imagine together what it would mean to escape the Assembly Line mindset and discover more faithful and more fruitful ways of framing what it means to follow Jesus together.

Chapter 2 (Fish Discover Water Last) begins to develop the tools we need to notice the default settings that quietly shape our expectations, understanding, emotions, and experience. As unlikely as it sounds, the way we live out our faith is shaped in significant ways by the metaphors we choose to live by. Noticing those default metaphors is the key to seeing new ways forward.

Chapter 3 (High Bar or Clay Jar?) gets at the basic Christian impulse to try and be more like Jesus. (I mean, what could possibly be wrong with that?) We'll discover that the way we naturally process self-improvement in terms of Up and Down leads to a place where we are constantly striving to do more and do better while comparing ourselves to others. But that kind of that striving Up to be like Jesus reverses the biblical direction of both salvation and sanctification, so we will need a way to rethink how we think about faith formation. If we focus on the Spirit's work to come Down and shape Jesus in us, we get a whole different set of obvious expectations, evaluations, and actions by default.

Chapter 4 (Relay Race or Rope Team?) looks at perhaps our most common way of framing the task of multi-generational faith development, something we often think of as "passing on the faith." While the dynamics of passing the torch or passing the baton aren't completely unbiblical, that way of thinking naturally fosters individual effort, unmet expectations, and rampant isolation. We'll try to expand our thinking about relational discipleship to include the dynamics of mountaineering on a rope team where we are all connected on the same journey.

At this crucial juncture in the book, we'll take a brief detour in order to get a better view of some important terrain we've covered so far. Chapter 5 (What You See is What You Get) uses the very different lived experiences of the Relay Race and Rope Team from Chapter 4 to notice how any specific *situation* has its own logic, expectations, and emotions. That **situational framing** becomes the key to understanding how our discipleship defaults shape our thoughts, feelings, evaluations, and actions before we even stop to think about it.

If you do pause long enough to notice how you are automatically framing your experience, you will need Wisdom to discern which filter is most appropriate for the situation in front of you. It's not simply a matter of right or wrong. Rather, you are trying to discern *which lens* to use in *this* situation.

Chapter 6 (Bank Vault or Banquet?) puts that situational thinking to test as we explore our default settings for the activity we commonly label "outreach." We'll discover how the basic orientation of In and Out can keep Jesus and outsiders as far apart as possible. To remedy our natural emphasis on boundary issues, we'll look for a way to imagine evangelism as a ministry of hospitality and crossing borders. We'll find Jesus not only at the *center* of our theology, but on the *leading edge* of our encounter with people not like us.

Chapter 7 (Pitched Battle or Pitched Tent?) takes that thinking one step further, into the arena we often imagine as Culture Wars. In the Church, as in our culture, our natural tendency is to frame any kind of disagreement as a kind of warfare: we not only reason about other people as enemies, we actually feel like we are under attack, and feel vindicated when we defend ourselves, or launch an aggressive counter-offensive.

While we do experience some people in our lives as enemies of the Gospel, we are also called to love our enemies, and practice the presence of Jesus with people who don't think like we do, or believe like we do, or vote like we do.

Noticing how Jesus came to *be with* us opens up new possibilities for us to simply *be with* others in ways that cultivate curiosity, reciprocity, and delight.

This book is just a beginning. The Conclusion (GPA or GPS? Where Do We Go from Here?) is a gracious invitation to keep moving forward without the burden of getting it right.

Noticing (let alone *changing*) your discipleship defaults isn't easy, so I'll try to keep the tone light. But it's also really important, so I'll use footnotes along the way, not only to add an aside here and there, but to ground what we are doing in a body of research that's all about how we draw obvious conclusions and live out our most basic ways of viewing the world. You don't have to follow the footnotes to get the most out of the book, but if you are wondering where in the world I came up with this stuff, I want to point you in the right direction.

Finally, rethinking our default ways of thinking is an exercise not only in humility but in dependence on Jesus. You'll find Scripture spread liberally throughout, not just in the footnotes or as a way of proof-texting a point, but as the heart of the project; we want to rethink in ways that lead us back to being more biblical, which will in turn lead us to a more joyful, vibrant, robust, and engaging life of faith in this beautiful-but-fallen world.

The writing of this book was done under the umbrella of daily prayer; prayers for my work as author and prayers for you, my readers. I think you will find what follows to be at times theoretical, and at times practical, but also thoroughly devotional. That is, I believe we cannot approach this topic well without careful attention to the work of the Spirit in us and in the Word embedded in the actual reading and writing of these words.

I don't claim anything like Scriptural authority, and I am happy to be wrong about any of this, as long as we keep talking and walking it out together. But I do invite you as a reader to adopt the same starting point I did as the author: would you begin your reading of this book with prayer? Not just here in the introduction, but anytime you pick it up?

Getting beyond our discipleship defaults to discover something more can only happen by the power of the Spirit working within us, whether we recognize and acknowledge it or not. But it's so much more life-giving to be consciously aware of how much we desperately need Jesus! Let's do that, together.

*Come, Holy Spirit, and shape us to be more like Jesus.
Make his thoughts, our thoughts. Make his heart, our heart.
Put the prayers of Jesus on our lips and the desires of Jesus in our guts,
that we might see, think, feel, imagine, and act a little more like
the Beloved Son, in whose name we pray. Amen.*

• • •

A Note on Chapter Icons, Intros, etc.

At the beginning of each chapter, and in the top margin of subsequent pages, you will find a pair of images that capture the central theme of each chapter: an industrial machine nut (Assembly Line) and a sun setting over a mountain (Adventure) in Chapter 1, for example, or the High Bar and Clay Jar in Chapter 3.

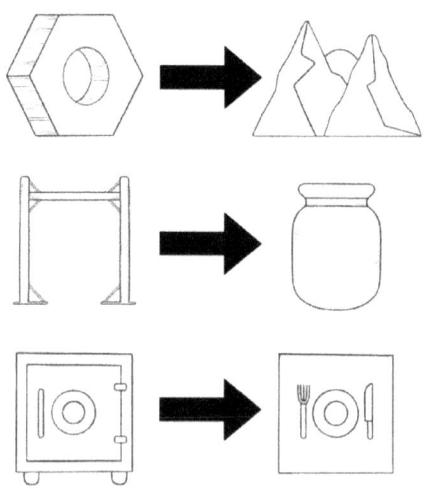

These icons aren't only a reminder of the big ideas in each chapter; they embody the fact that **big changes in perspective can come by making even small adjustments.** The setting sun mirrors the hole of the industrial nut; the clay jar fits nicely inside the negative space of the high bar; that banquet plate looks like it came directly off the front of the bank vault.

You probably would have noticed all of that on your own, but I find that *what goes without saying* often *shouldn't*. Once you see how the icons for each chapter relate to each other, you'll have captured a major theme of the entire book: **changing our discipleship defaults boils down to taking our standard models and shifting them, just slightly, so they align more directly with the way the Bible imagines faith and following.** That's the goal of this whole experiment; the chapter icons are guide posts along the way.

In concert with these icons, most chapters begin with a kind of introductory overview: a brief description of our typical default settings, some good reasons why we think that way, a few unintended consequences, and a thumbnail sketch of how we might imagine something more. Every chapter that includes this overview also ends with "This Changes Everything," a reference table of the key shifts in thinking that come with adjusting your default governing image.

Along with Chapter Summaries and Reflection Questions, these features provide a quick way to review the key insights of each chapter. If you are trying to remember something you read, you might also consult the list of works cited or the Index of Metaphors or Scripture Index at the end.

You might not need all of the overviews or summaries or group discussion questions. That's fine; use what you find helpful and move on. But noticing (let alone changing) our default assumptions about faith and following is a challenging business, so all of these different tools are an attempt to make that task both a little easier and a little more fun.

• • •

Summary of the Introduction

It's OK to long for something more in your experience of faith and following. The way we have been imagining the Church and what it means to live a Christian life has led us to where we are today. If we want to get a different result, we will need to rethink *how we think* about things like Church or discipleship or Christian living. It's not easy to notice our own default assumptions. But if we can, we have a chance to discover more faithful, more biblical, and more beautiful ways of reframing and imagining—and therefore living out—what it means to follow Jesus. All of the different tools included in each chapter are simply means to support that end.

For Further Reflection

Do you, or any people you know, relate to the *longing for something more* expressed in the introduction?

This assessment of our current thinking about Church or Christian living can seem somewhat negative or convicting, but also hopeful. Did you agree with this evaluation? Do know other people who would resonate with this introduction?

Which seemed stronger in the Introduction: dissatisfaction or hope?
Which is stronger in your life right now, dissatisfaction or hope?

What Bible stories or verses come to mind when you reflect on this introduction?
How might this section lead you to pray? Take time to pray like that.

Chapter 1

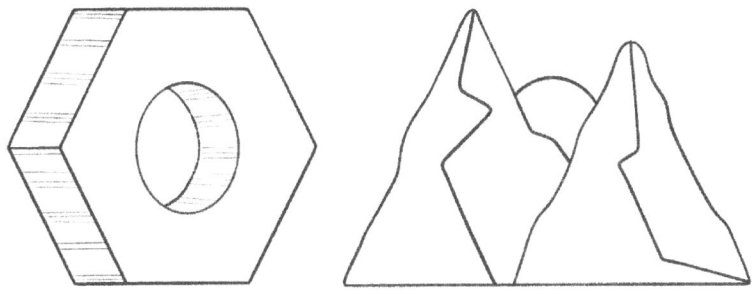

Assembly Line or Adventure?
Something More than "Making Disciples"

Our Default Setting: We typically imagine "disciple making" as a standardized process, run by the trained professionals, designed to produce a consistent end product as efficiently as possible.

Some Good Reasons for Our Default: With limited time, staff, and resources, congregations need to be efficient with their new member process. Making sure new believers or new members get the same basic content allows us to safeguard the doctrine of the Church. Plus, a standardized method has worked well in the past (in a basically church-going culture).

Some Unintended Consequences: New people are processed by professional church staff as quickly as possible (while still achieving an acceptable minimum result). Nonprofessionals are expected to bring the raw materials of "the nations" to the location where disciples are "made" (the church building). In order to maintain efficiency, anyone who does not fit within the scope of the standardized process is allowed to drop out or drift away. Once the process is complete, new disciples are seen as (mostly) finished products, with no real need for ongoing support.

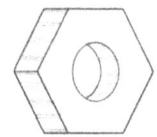

Something More: If you want to shift from Assembly Line assumptions to an Adventure mindset, move the work of *discipling* from a select few professionals to a journey everyone can join and enjoy. Create an expectation that real faith development and life change happen outside the walls of the church, in an ongoing process over time. Focus the professional time in the official space on training non-professionals for their calling outside the building.

• • •

The Great Commission

"Go therefore and make disciples of all nations …" (Matthew 28:19). Those are the words of Jesus. The Great Commission. The core of who we are and what we are supposed to be about. How we imagine the Great Commission will affect almost every area of our faith. Why would we ever need to rethink the central mission of the Church, the primary marching orders for every individual Christian? Those words seem so natural; the response so *obvious* …

I am *not* suggesting we rethink the words of Jesus. But we do need to take a closer look at how we imagine—and therefore live out—what we think Jesus *meant* by those words. The roles, expectations, goals, parameters, evaluations, possibilities, and hoped-for outcomes we have unconsciously imposed on the Great Commission have built a construct called "Making Disciples" that we hardly notice because it seems so natural and obvious.

It's just the air we breathe, the water we swim in. And that natural and obvious way of imagining the Great Commission is actually hurting the Church.

The Great Assembly Line

By the year 1913, the Ford plant in Highland Park, Michigan was producing a Model T every three minutes. The revolutionary manufacturing model called an "assembly line" worked so efficiently and so well, there was only one paint color that would dry fast enough to keep up with production. That's the origin of

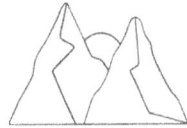

Henry Ford's famous quip (from his autobiography, *My Life and Work*): "Any customer can have a car painted any color that he wants, so long as it is black!"

What was revolutionary in 1913 is commonplace today; an industrial, assembly line, mass-production mentality permeates our everyday lives. We interact almost exclusively with mass-produced merchandise—from cars, to clothes, to computers, to hamburgers. When was the last time you drove, wore, or consumed something that was crafted, sewn, or cooked individually, by hand, from scratch?

Mass production is an ordinary part of our ordinary lives, so much so that when Jesus says, "Go, therefore, and *make* disciples *of* all nations ... and I am with you always," we, who know almost nothing but mass production, hear Jesus say, "Go, therefore, and *mass-produce* standardized *end products* out of the *raw materials* of the nations ... and I will be your assembly line foreman, to the very end of the age."

I'm not saying we *try* to hear Jesus that way; I am saying that, without trying, you and I, as products of our culture, hear the command to "make disciples" and naturally filter the Great Commission through the metaphor of an assembly line. When that happens—when we hear the Great Commission as "mass-produce disciple doodads"—then something important gets lost.

Have you ever been in a Ford plant? Or any modern manufacturing facility? Even if you don't have first-hand familiarity, you probably know how an assembly line works. **An assembly line focuses on *how fast* you can produce the *exact same end product*.** In order to minimize mistakes and maximize efficiency, everything is standardized: everything is done the exact same way, over and over again, every single time.

When I was in high school, up in Flint, Michigan, I worked for an automotive supply plant off and on, so I can tell you from personal experience that it is more *efficient* and *cost-effective* to trash an individual product with a problem than to go back and try fix that one, solitary unit.

If a thingamajig comes down the assembly line and it's not put together quite right, you junk it. Why? Because it takes way too much time to go back and fix it. **The assembly line cannot tolerate any deviation from the norm.**

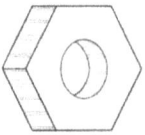

And that's why it works. That's why the line is fast and effective. That's why the foreman is watching: to make sure you throw that defective part away, because the line must keep moving forward at all costs. *"If the line isn't moving, we're losing money."* That mentality was drilled into everyone on the floor.

My usual job on the line was to unpack, and then repack, spark plugs and oil filters and y-splices and terminal butt splices. I took them out of boxes that had Chinese written on them, and put them into boxes with English on them. (Makes you wonder, doesn't it?) That was my job. I put them on pallets, and stretch-wrapped them, and sent them out the door.

And when my shift was over, I didn't care what happened to any of those auto parts. I didn't care what kind of car they went into. I didn't care what shelf they ended up on. I was done with them! When I'm done with my shift, I go on with my weekend. I didn't have an ongoing connection to that end product any more than the guy driving the delivery truck did: the semi driver would always drop off pallets full of spark plugs and oil filters as fast as he could, and then get on with the rest of his day.

From start to finish, mass production demands that anyone who is part of the process does their job as fast as possible, in isolation, and then moves on.

Mass Producing Disciple Doodads

When we hear "*make* disciples" in our cultural context, we naturally and automatically tend to go into production mode. Because mass production is the mode we know best, we tend to filter the process of disciple-making through the inferences, values, and uncritical assumptions of the assembly line.

I don't think we do it on purpose. I do think it is hurting the Church.

If "making disciples of all nations" becomes "taking raw materials and producing a disciple doodad," then we will uncritically assume we should focus on *how quickly we can produce the same end product.*

The obvious outcome and unquestionable goal of our assembly line is to produce people who look like us, and pray like us, confess like us, and theologize like us. And in order to minimize theological mistakes and

maximize pastoral efficiency, the discipleship process logically becomes standardized, professionalized, one-size-fits-all, over and over and over again. Every. Single. Time.

We naturally tend to take whomever we can get and let the *professional* line workers run them through the same standard, *efficient* process they always use, reasonably expecting to get *the same basic product* out the other end.

When I show up at my local disciple-making factory, I unsurprisingly tend to sit back and ride the conveyer belt through worship, trusting that the professional doodad-makers will do their thing to me.

Once I am out the door, I don't give it a second thought. I don't even consider giving it a second thought. Why would I? **Disciple-making activity obviously belongs in the disciple-making building.**

If I happen to encounter someone "out there" in my real life who needs discipling, I may try to take a few whacks at them with some of the same standardized techniques I saw the professionals use on me last Sunday, but most likely, if I see someone who needs Jesus out there in the world, my natural goal is to get them into the factory and onto the line, where the professional discipler-makers can do their job.

It's so obvious! I bring the natural resource of the nations, and put those natural resources on the conveyor belt of the local congregation, and hope for the best. My job is done; I can get on with the rest of my weekend.

And the "discipling professionals" are crazy enough to agree to and implicitly encourage that plan! Pastors and other church professionals naturally tend toward a standardized, one-size-fits-all Christian education process, that happens *inside* the church building, because *if you're producing a disciple doodad, the faster, the better.*

A standardized process is obviously more *efficient*, and therefore, an *unquestionably* better use of the pastor's time. (Efficiency is a core value we uncritically adopt from our consumer culture.)

I know this because I have been a professional disciple-maker. I can think and act like I'm on an assembly line sometimes. I am crazy enough to have

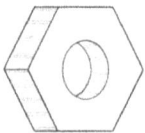

taught standardized, one-size-fits-all new member courses. In fact, I was the one who standardized them!

I want to be different. For years in the parish, I was trying to be different. But when you are on the line, it's hard to evaluate your own uncritical assumptions. And the conveyer belt just keeps on moving...

What really bothers me, what nags at me in my busyness and pains my heart (when I let it)—what really makes me question our typical approach to this whole discipleship thing is the fact that *it is more effective and cost efficient* to trash an individual with a problem than to take the time to go back and get it right. It's better *for the line* to just keep production going.

There will always be the ones who *almost* get connected; who catch a glimpse of discipleship, but falter; who start to know Jesus but then seem to drift off. And an assembly line mentality demands that, when they drift away, we as a church—and I as a pastor—let them go. They aren't worth the extra effort, because extra effort takes time; time you don't have, because the next new round of new member classes starts next week.

The natural logic of the assembly line means that **my relationship with any individual product is designed to be as short as humanly possible.**

Get 'em in, get 'em out, as fast as you can.

I can watch that widget go on down the line and out the door, but what do I care? The delivery truck just dropped off more raw resources at the docking bay (and got out of here as fast as possible).

The next doodad is already on the conveyor belt in front of me; I obviously have to get back to work...

At least, that's how I have seen this mass-discipleship paradigm play out in my life and ministry. I don't think you have to live within a ninety-minute radius of the Motor City (like I do) for Assembly Line thinking to sneak into your default way of making disciples. Efficiency, standardization, professionalization, and other industrial values permeate our culture in ways so pervasive they can be hard to see.

At the same time, I know that not everyone grew up in a congregation that tended toward a standardized New Member Class for all new members. For

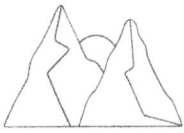

some churches, *any kind* of onboarding method would be more than they are used to, and an Assembly Line may feel like an improvement! Better a standardized process than no process at all.

For others, the problem is not that professional church workers can't afford to spend time on individuals; it's the exact opposite. In extreme cases, personal interest in faith formation can become controlling, domineering, or even coercive. Those kinds of unhealthy and even abusive systems might be more likely to prey on the weak than leave them on the factory floor.

Still other followers may recognize something about that Assembly Line mentality, but not know it from personal experience. In their own lives, discipleship was modeled as mutual, ongoing, healthy growth into deeper dependence on Jesus. Thank God whenever and wherever that happens.

But if you have seen manipulation passed off as discipleship, or you have lacked any kind of support from your local congregation, or if you, at times, like me, at times, have been in the business of dropping off raw materials at your local disciple-making factory, or mass-producing standardized disciple doodads without even realizing that's what you were doing, then pause for a moment and take a deep breath! I've got good news.

None of that is what Jesus actually *meant* when he said, "Go and *make disciples* of all nations." In fact, "make disciples," isn't exactly what Jesus even *said*.

What Jesus Actually Said

I guess I understand why our most common English translations[2] give us "*make* disciples of all nations." The problem is, when we 21st-century North Americans *make* something *out of* something else, we just naturally get into a production line mentality.

---

[2] The ESV, NIV, NKJV, NRSV, and NASB all have some version of "Go, therefore" or "Therefore, go" and "make disciples of all nations." The Message (of course) has "Go out and train everyone you meet, far and near, in this way of life..." Which, really, isn't half bad, as long as the "training" is a kind of apprenticeship. (We Modern Westerners have turned even education into a mass production assembly line...)

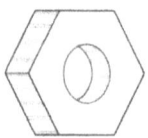

But disciples aren't an end product, a doodad you *make*; "discipling" is a *verb*—an activity you *do*. Jesus isn't commanding us to *produce standardized thingamabobs*; he is commanding us to *engage others on a journey* of following.

Jesus *actually* said, "Going, *disciple* the nations…"

And **when you turn "discipling" back into an *activity* instead of an *end product*, it makes all the difference in the world!**

For Jesus, and for the people of his day and culture, the verb, the *activity* of "being a disciple," meant you had a strong and personal relationship with one specific teacher, or sage, or master.

Your job description as a "disciple" was literally to walk with, and listen to, and eat with, and eavesdrop on, and journey next to your master so that his words became your words; his understanding of Scripture became your understanding of Scripture; his way of praying became your way of praying; his faith became your faith.

The process didn't happen overnight. The expedition didn't always follow the same route or routine. The journey could get long, or complicated, or even treacherous, but being a disciple *by definition* meant sticking close to your teacher wherever he went.

So when Jesus says, "Look! I am with you always!" he isn't promising to be the line foreman making sure you are dropping off enough raw materials or cranking out the right kind of disciple products at the right pace.

Instead, Jesus is reaffirming a discipling relationship with you, a *master-to-disciple* relationship: personal, specific, unique, and above all, ongoing.[3]

---

[3] The Hebrew word "rabbi" literally translates as "my master." The official title and position of Rabbi is a post-70 AD development, but Jewish tradition speaks of teachers who talked and argued and discipled on the road a hundred years before Jesus.

My favorite example of what I think is going on in the master-disciple relationship happens Easter evening on the way to the town of Emmaus (Luke 24). Opening your home to a wise teacher, being covered in his dust (either walking on the road or sitting at his feet), and being thirsty for his words—that's what we see in the relationship between the Master Jesus and his traveling disciples. That's the kind of ongoing relationship Jesus desires to have with you. (It's also a description of the master-disciple relationship that apparently predates Jesus by about 150 years.)

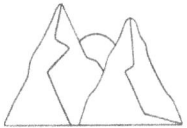

When Jesus says, "I am with you always," he is inviting you to keep following him, learning from him, eating with him, being molded and shaped by him, so his words more and more become your words; his understanding of Scripture more and more becomes your understanding of Scripture; his prayers become your prayers; his faith more and more, day by day, step by step, becomes your faith, too.

Jesus loves you like that.

Jesus wants to hang out with you day in and day out.

Jesus recommits himself to you, to be present and active in your very own personal, tailor-made, handcrafted discipleship journey.

You are not a standardized thingamabob. One size does not fit all.

You are not a standardized thingamabob; and Jesus doesn't want you to produce standardized thingamabobs. That's not how it works.

Disciple the Nations

Not once did Jesus ever say, "Anyone can make a disciple any color he wants ... as long as it's white." Instead, Jesus gives you the command: *disciple* the nations. All of them. Every single one of them.

Jesus says, "Make my Church a Revelation 7 Church: with every tribe, people, nation, language group. Don't try to make a thousand identical disciple doodads. As you go, disciple the nations in all of their variety and diversity and beautiful differences from each other and from you."

To disciple the nations, you just find one or two individually unique people. Or three. Or maybe seven. (Jesus had twelve, you know. Twelve is too many for me. He's Jesus. I'll take two or three.)

According to the logic of *discipling* (the activity, not the end product), you will have to walk with them; and sit with them; and eat with them; and joke with them; and talk with them. You will naturally let them look over your shoulder, and eavesdrop on your prayers. You let them see the tears when you grieve. You invite them over for a beer to help you celebrate. That's how discipleship works: in mutual relationship, over time.

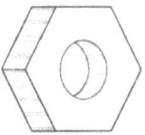

If discipleship is actually sharing life on a journey that sometimes has twists and turns, and sometimes has dead ends, and sometimes significant detours—if discipleship is about putting in time and doing life with someone in a daily kind of way, then **there's no way that the professional staff of any congregation can take care of all of the** *discipling* **that needs to take place.**

Why do we need to rethink "making disciples"? Because the uncritical assumptions that belong to mass production tend to run the table on our imagining, feeling, and decision making when we turn the activity of *discipling* (walking with) into an action of *production* (creating a standardized product).

As long as "manufacturing an end product" is the only way we process "making disciples," we will only be able to imagine possibilities that involve a standardized, professionalized, efficient process designed to produce reliable results by doing the same thing every time.

To reimagine the Great Commission in more faithful, beautiful, effective, and joyful ways, we need to get away from discipleship as a standardized process performed by professionals. For the sake of our future, for the sake of our neighbors and our grandkids, we need a different way of framing and filtering our thoughts, feelings, and actions when it comes to discipleship.

Imagining a Walking-With Community

I think we might actually have to imagine a *community*, a group of people together. Let's call that local community "church." And let's say these people are committed to walking with each other on the journey as they try to figure out what it means to follow Jesus together, day by day, one step at a time.

In that kind of community, we might even be willing to say we're not so focused on efficiency, or results, or numbers that we can't go out of our way to walk with people who take a little extra time; people who don't automatically believe what we want them to; people who don't look like us or talk like us; people who otherwise would end up on the production line floor.

This isn't some new revelation!

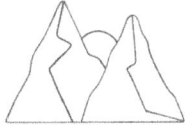

I already see this way of imagining (and therefore living out) the Great Commission alive in the Church. I have seen people go out of their way to make sure everyone feels welcome, everyone is included, everyone knows they are unique, and loved, and invited to take a next step.

That way of imagining the life of the Church in the world needs to become our *go-to*, our default setting, the filter that establishes the actions, feelings, thoughts, and goals of discipling.

There will always be a place for large gatherings; Jesus also taught the crowds. But when it comes to how we imagine personal development in faith and following, **the logic of *walking with* needs to displace the logic of *mass production* as our natural default setting.**

I think one key might be to keep pushing discipling relationships outside of the building, beyond Sunday morning, and into the daily lives of every single follower. There is more wrestling and conversation and discovery that Jesus wants to happen through the Church than can possibly cross a staff person's desk or fit in one hour a week.

What's the alternative to professional disciple-making? We all have to disciple—that is, *walk with*—the people right in front of us, so we can be part of the adventure, the wrestling, the conversation, and the discovery that helps individuals, one or two at a time, take a next step following Jesus.

In the end, that kind of messy, confusing, loving, sinful-but-forgiven, *walking with* community is going to be a whole lot more fun to be around than a group of line workers who can't wait to finish their shift and get on with their weekend, or a bunch of truck drivers who drop off the raw materials at the factory as quickly as possible and leave the "real" work to the paid professionals.

The obvious right answers, natural outcomes, clear dividing lines, and unquestionable goals of an assembly line distort the Gospel and burden both professional church workers and everyday disciples.

But you and I aren't in the business of producing doodads.

We are called to *disciple* the nations.

We get to walk with people on the adventure of discovering what Jesus is going to do next. And we aren't limited to a particular building or time or

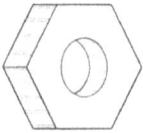

standardized process. We get to share in the unique stories of real people in their unique lives and watch for how Jesus meets them right where they are, and explore where Jesus is inviting them to head next.

You and I aren't called to produce standardized, one-size-fits-all discipleship doodads. We get to experience the adventure *discipling* the nations.

How awesome is that!?

Changing the Assembly Line in Midstride

One of the congregations I served as pastor had a long-standing tradition of celebrating the Sacrament in every worship service, every single Sunday. They also had a long-standing tradition of continuous flow distribution; that is, everyone queued up in a single-file line and came forward to receive the bread and wine, one person at a time.

Continuous flow distribution, like any church practice, has both advantages and disadvantages, and while it's not my favorite way to do it, I had been warned both by Seminary professors and by my own congregational experience that messing with a congregation's communion practice is kicking a wasp hive looking for honey. So while I gently broached the subject in leadership meetings, the entrenchment seemed high and I had plenty of other things to think about as we moved forward together.

So, for better or worse, single file continuous flow was the way we *always* did Communion at that church. It became part of the background noise; part of the furniture; part of the water I was swimming in as pastor. I didn't think about it, or even really *notice* it anymore...

Until the day I preached on the difference between *making discipleship doodads on an assembly line* and *walking with others on a journey of faith*. After the sermon, the service continued with Communion (like always). About halfway through, one of our Elders came up in the single file distribution line. The rest of his young family had already moved through. I said, "Take and eat," placing the host in his open hands; with a wry smile, he replied: "I sure feel like I'm on an assembly line right now."

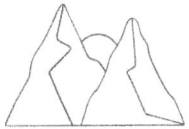

Ouch! That hit home! I had asked the congregation to view their world differently, and this Elder had done just that. Once you see single file continuous flow communion through the lens of an assembly line, you can't unsee it. (I'm not saying continuous flow distribution is wrong everywhere and always; just that, as part of our default settings, that practice had become obvious, natural, and unquestionable at my own congregation, with some negative results.)

Now, I could have gotten a little defensive at that point—I mean, it wasn't *my* idea to do it this way, and what can you do with a zinger like that in the middle of a service anyway?—but thankfully I was moved to take immediate action. We had already been talking about "running small experiments" and "taking small next steps" as individuals and as a congregation, and I think that helped with what happened next.

You see, I stopped the service right then and there. **Once you see the assembly line, you can't just keep it going.** I actually interrupted the organist. When the music ground to a halt, I told the congregation what the Elder had just said about being on an assembly line, and announced that we would run a small, spontaneous experiment in worship. The change might not work, but we would try it for a few weeks and see how it goes.

I told people to keep the flow moving, but to come up in groups of two or three, or to approach as a family, so that no one communes alone. Then the organist started playing again, and the service continued.

We had Communion at the next service, too (remember, we had Communion at *every* worship service), and I announced the experiment after the sermon, so we ran the experiment in that service, too. Over the next few weeks, we made some minor adjustments, but from that day forward we always celebrated the Lord's Supper in groups of two to seven as a way of living out a vision of discipleship. We valued walking together over a standardized, professionalized, impersonal conveyor belt process.

We changed our communion practice on the fly without congregational backlash or upheaval. How? The language of "running an experiment" and "small next steps" set us up to be open to incremental change; the Spirit moved

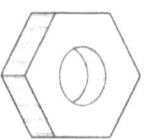

through the Word; the Adventure metaphor helped us notice the default assumptions that promoted Assembly Line values; and when we saw an alternative option, we took it.

Maybe that's how we should usually try to affect change in the Church: notice the metaphors that make the status quo seem unquestionable and inevitable, and then change the lens through which we experience following Jesus so that something more vibrant, more faithful, and more fun begins to seem natural and obvious, instead. **Change the metaphor before you change the practice.** (It worked, too; at least in this one situation.)

You Never Walk Alone

I recently had the chance to tell that story in a retreat setting. It has been a few years, and I am not a pastor at that congregation anymore, but one of the women at the retreat told me afterwards that *she was there* in worship, the day we made that change. In fact, she had been standing in line when I stopped distribution to change our communion practice.

She told me how startled she was when I called a halt to the communion line. She told me about the moment of panic she had as she wondered who would commune with her, since she was alone in worship (as usual).

She smiled as she remembered the warm invitation from people around her to come to the Lord's Supper with them. "And every Sunday after that," she said, "I have felt more at home in worship than I ever did before. When I come to a service by myself, I know there will be people ready to welcome me. I don't have to be alone."

That's the difference between living out a Christian Assembly Line and belonging to a Walking With community who are on this Adventure together: on the Adventure of Following Jesus, you never walk alone.

• • •

Summary of Chapter 1: Assembly Line or Adventure?

The logic of an assembly line tends to filter our assumptions about "making disciples" so that the process is standardized, professionalized, and efficient to the point that the process cannot tolerate deviation. The logic of "walking with" requires more people focused on discipling in more places than the church building and opens up the possibilities of what discipling might look like.

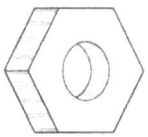

This Changes Everything

	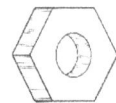 The Assembly Line	 The Adventure
Jesus	The foreman who makes sure you keep the line moving.	The Master who leads and teaches on the way, as you go.
The Church	The factory where professionals do the standardized discipling.	A "walking with" community that knows we follow Jesus better when we follow him together.
The World	The raw resources you bring to the discipling factory.	A place to be explored; people to walk with, as you go.
The Goal	Produce disciple doodads as efficiently as possible as long as they meet the standards.	Keep taking small next steps in the direction Jesus is leading. Invite others to walk with you.
My Role	Go through the standardized process as quickly as possible to become a finished product. Bring raw materials to the factory for the professionals to disciple.	I am a follower first, but then also someone who walks with other people. I am not a doodad and I don't produce doodads. My adventure is tailor-made.
Key Thinking	The process must be standardized, professionalized, and efficient. The line must keep moving.	I wonder where Jesus will lead us next! The journey of discovery doesn't end.

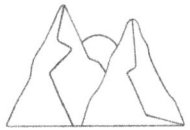

For Further Reflection

What aspects of your congregation's ministry are "standardized" or "professionalized"? In what ways have those aspects worked well? When do they not work as well?

Share a story of a time when you experienced a "walking with" relationship that helped you discover something new over time.

Another way of thinking about discipling is as **an apprenticeship**. What kinds of uncritical assumptions, obvious goals, or hoped-for outcomes belong to the Apprentice frame? How would Apprentice assumptions filter our discipleship experience? Consider specifically the following:

An Apprenticeship

Jesus	
The Church	
The World	
The Goal	
My Role	
Key Thinking	

Chapter 2

Fish Discover Water Last
Rethinking How We Think

What's Natural and Obvious (and Mostly Invisible)

Noticing your own assumption about what's natural and obvious is especially difficult. That's because your assumptions seem so, well, *natural and obvious*. You don't *intend* to value efficiency and standardization when it comes to spiritual formation; you just *do*, because those values are all around you.

I remember a comic strip I saw way back in high school: two small fish are just hanging out when an older fish swims by and asks, in passing, "How's the water today, boys?" After the more experienced fish has moved on, one of the younger fish has a startling thought: "What's '*water*'?"[1]

We face a similar situation as we try to think about *how we automatically think about* our lives of faith. The "obvious" right answers, "natural" outcomes, "clear" dividing lines, and "unquestionable" goals of our current cultural iteration of Christianity are all based on fundamental assumptions about faith and following. "Making disciples" as if people were doodads on a conveyor belt is just one of the possible paradigms that naturally become

---

[1] Yes, I am aware that David Foster Wallace told a version of this joke at Kenyon College in a 2005 commencement speech titled, "This is Water." All I can say is, he must have seen the same comic strip growing up as I did. I didn't know of the Wallace quote until I was trying to track down that comic. (Google the speech; it's worth a listen.)

part of "the way we (*obviously*) do things around here." Along with "making disciples," other religious-sounding constructs like "trying to be like Jesus" or "passing on the faith" or "outreach" or "defending the truth" all function as a network of default settings, part of the water we swim in—water we hardly notice because it's always there.

Our uncritical assumptions about faith and following make our standard Christian answers *feel* obvious, typical outcomes *appear* natural, dividing lines *look* clear, and goals *seem* unquestionable. That's why fish discover water last; it takes a moment of clarity even to notice that something needs to be discovered in the first place.

Thinking critically about our uncritical thinking goes against our natural wiring. But that **self-reflection is essential, especially if our automatic answers, assumed goals, and natural assumptions are unintentionally clouding the Gospel.** We need some tools to help us rethink how we think.

I'm not pretending to be the more experienced fish in this scenario; I'm just saying, I think our most prevalent and most natural ways of imagining discipleship are all wet. I'm not accusing you of swimming in the wrong direction; I'm saying, I think there is something wrong with our pond.

We're flopping around in shallow water, half-suffocated and getting nowhere fast. But Jesus came to bring life, life to the full. Jesus pours out living water. Jesus wants to provide so much more than we ask or imagine.

And we're stuck in the same old stifling routine that has sucked the life out of our experience, swimming the same old hamster wheel (pardon the mixed metaphor) that has gotten us where we are today: feeling stuck in the same old patterns, but without the tools to imagine something more.

The industrialization of our core mission to "make disciples" is just the tip of the metaphorical iceberg. So now what?

An Experiment in Assumptions

A few years back, a group of social scientists and cognitive linguists got together to think about the way we think. They wanted to understand the

dynamics that shape and reinforce our uncritical assumptions, behind the scenes. They were fish discovering water.

Their work was quite ingenious (and more detailed than we can cover here) but one of their experiments in particular will help. The scientists handed two groups of people *identical* information with one important difference: the scientists altered *the way they framed* the exact same data in order to test how your imagination affects your interpretation.

In other words, **how do the default assumptions you use to understand a situation affect how you make basic decisions about that situation?**

The scientists shared identical data (facts) about crime statistics in a fictional city. "Wild beast" language filtered the data in the first test case:

> Crime is a **wild beast** *preying* on the city of Addison. The crime rate in the once peaceful city has steadily increased over the past three years. In fact, these days it seems that crime is *lurking in* every neighborhood. In 2004, 46,177 crimes were reported compared to more than 55,000 reported in 2007. The rise in violent crime is particularly alarming. In 2004, there were 330 murders in the city, in 2007, there were over 500.

Based on that report, the test group was asked to brainstorm solutions to the rise in crime. You can probably imagine what happens next...

Before I tell you about this first group's proposed solutions, let me introduce you to the second test group. The scientists also asked this second group to brainstorm some actionable solutions to the problem of crime in the fictional city of Addison, but the report they gave the second group looked very slightly different. (I've put the only differences in the two reports in bold.)

> Crime is a **virus** *infecting* the city of Addison. The crime rate in the once peaceful city has steadily increased over the past three years. In fact, these days it seems that crime is *plaguing* every neighborhood. In 2004, 46,177 crimes were reported compared to more than 55,000 reported in 2007. The rise in violent crime is particularly alarming. In 2004, there were 330 murders in the city, in 2007, there were over 500.

The specific parameters and comprehensive results of this experiment are detailed in a 2011 paper titled, "Metaphors We Think With: The Role of

Metaphor in Reasoning."[2] The metaphor of *Crime as a Wild Beast* in the first report has shifted to the metaphor of *Crime as a Virus* in the second report; and *that's the only difference* in the reports!

When you change the metaphor, you change the way the question is framed; you reset the filter; you realign what seems natural and obvious, what seems probable or possible, what counts as winning or losing. In other words, when you change the metaphor, you *reimagine* crime in ways that change how you *naturally think, feel, and act* in relation to crime and criminals.

The people in the Wild Beast test group brainstormed all kinds of *obvious* answers to a rise in crime. Their answers were consistent with the logic of a wild beast loose in the city. This first test group was statistically much more likely to suggest solutions that required better means of *hunting down* perpetrators. The results they anticipated were more likely to involve *locking up* the threat in a *cage* in order to *protect* the innocent from harm.

The Virus test group, on the other hand, saw the data (and the world) very differently. Because a different metaphor filtered their imaginations, their basic assumptions about the data changed. They were fish swimming in very different water. These people were much more likely to propose solutions that spent money on *finding the root cause* of the crime infection and working on *treatments* that led to a *cure*, including things like social reform or an information campaign. Incarceration was treated under the logic of *quarantine*, and for the Virus test group, the *rehabilitation* of the criminal was as obvious and natural as protecting the innocent.

Neither of these perspectives is inherently right or wrong; but they are very different ways of viewing the world that lead to very different "obvious" answers, "natural" outcomes, and "unquestionable" goals.

What looks like a subtle change in framing created a blatant change in the perception of the problem. That change in perception led to very different suggested solutions. Whether you think about crime as a Wild Beast or as a Virus fundamentally filters how you perceive the data, and what *possible actions*

---

[2] Thibodeau, Paul H and Lera Boroditsky. PLoS ONE 6(2): e16782. Available online at: https://doi.org/10.1371/journal.pone.0016782.

are even available for you to consider. That shift in metaphor has the power to shift your way of thinking, reasoning, feeling, imagining, and behaving.

Just the Facts, Ma'am

The way you frame any issue changes the way people will understand the dynamics of the issue. And here's the kicker: while some people in both test groups *noticed* the metaphor framing the question, **they completely discounted the power of metaphor to shape their uncritical assumptions.** The study notes:

> Despite the clear influence of the metaphor, we found that participants generally identified the crime statistics, which were the same for both groups, and not the metaphor, as the most influential aspect of the report. These findings suggest that metaphors can influence how people conceptualize and in turn approach solving an important social issue, even if people don't explicitly perceive the metaphor as being especially influential.

The participants seemed to think, by and large, that they were being influenced by "just the facts." As they reflected on their experience of the data, it *felt to them* like *the statistics* carried the most weight. Even when these fish noticed the water, the water didn't seem very important…

When the test subjects were asked to give a reason for their decisions, they did what we all do, all the time: they created a story that explained their past actions in ways that seemed plausible to their present mindset. They reported, after the fact, that the statistics were the key factor that shaped their thinking about crime. But that can't be right: the statistics were *the same* in both reports. The most influential part of the experience had to be something else.

Although *the facts* seem like a reasonable thing to base your conclusion on, *the logic of wild beasts and viruses* framed and filtered the facts, so that some decisions seemed natural and obvious while others were rejected or ignored. Once you see crime as a Virus, you will naturally evaluate the statistical data differently and come up with different *obvious* responses than if you imagine crime as a Wild Beast. **When it comes to uncritical assumptions, the metaphor makes the difference.**

Reframing How We Follow

I can't overstate the importance of uncritical assumptions when it comes to following Jesus. If you want to grow in your relationship with Jesus and live out your faith in your everyday life, then you can't discount the power of metaphor to shape what seems natural and obvious to you, what actions and emotions seem appropriate in your workday or in your prayer life, and what solutions or outcomes seem most reasonable (or even possible) to you.

Even if it doesn't feel like it, the metaphors you typically live by have the power to shape the way you think, reason, feel, evaluate the past, view the future, and behave in the present.[3] **As long as we are unaware of the water we swim in, we will only imagine possibilities that naturally fit with what seems obvious and natural in our current status quo.**

Maybe you could recognize the efficient Assembly Line metaphor for faith formation from your own church experience. If you did, you likely also felt that something as simple as talking about "making disciples" instead of "discipling people" is pretty insignificant. Metaphors don't seem to matter.

But the words we use are a window into the structure of our thinking. As long as a paradigm of efficiency, standardization, and professionalization is running the show, you will naturally come to obvious conclusions about who should teach the New Member Class, or how long it should take, or where you should hold it; and all of those answers will align with the logic and emotions embedded in the Assembly Line. The metaphor makes all the difference.

That's true of every aspect of the life of faith. If I get in an argument with a friend or family member about going to church and I imagine I am supposed to be "passing the faith on to the next generation," what I think is happening—what I am experiencing, what I am hoping for and afraid of, my goals for the argument and the emotions I experience during those exchanges, what counts as success or failure—*everything about my emotion, logic, and action* in that moment is shaped by the logic of relay races and batons.

---

[3] In fact, one of the most influential books in the field is called *Metaphors We Live By.* (Written by George Lakoff and Mark Johnson. Make sure you get the 2003 updated version.)

If, instead, I think that other person is "on my rope" as we are on this "journey" of faith together, the situation shifts dramatically. The facts haven't changed: I still want them to go to church and they still don't want to go. But my list of options, reasonable responses, even the kinds of emotions I am experiencing and the kinds of prayers I am praying have all shifted. My expectations are different. My actions are different. Framing the relationship in terms of Journey rather than Relay Race changes what I see as possible, without me even being aware of the metaphor's influence.

Think of another common way for framing the faith: if I see the world around me as a "threat," if I think the Church needs to be "protected" from the culture, if the people who don't know Jesus in my life are fundamentally "outsiders," then even if I want to "witness" to them or "win souls" for the Kingdom, my feelings, thoughts, expectations, and evaluations will be shaped by the dynamics of Containers and Warfare: you divide the inside from the outside, and then protect what's inside from what's outside.

If, on the other hand, I see the world around me as a "field ripe for harvest," as a place where Jesus is active, as the setting for an "adventure of discovery" and you never know where the Spirit is going to show up, or how the "seed" is going to do its work, then my emotions, expectations, desired outcomes, and imagined possibilities will shift.

If the primary mode I use to engage people who don't know Jesus is *Hospitality* rather than *Warfare*, I will have different kinds of conversations in which I speak of Jesus in ways that are very different from "mounting an offensive" or even "defending my position." I will be much less likely to "defend the faith" and much more likely to invite someone who doesn't believe like I do to "come and see."

What counts as success and failure will change. What I think I am doing "out in the world" will change. How I pray for other people, the kinds of sins I confess, what gives me joy, what gives me hope—all of those things will change based on whether I see faith as a "fortress" that is "under attack" or as a "journey" or "banquet" to which all are invited. None of the people around me change, but my attitude, actions, and reasoning about those people change.

One of the most important things you can do as a follower of Jesus is to pay attention to the metaphors you live by. The best way to rethink how you think about your life of faith is to notice what actions seem obvious (or even *possible*) to you. The decisions *you make* will be limited by the decisions *you see in front of you*.

Even when metaphors are filtering your uncritical assumptions (and therefore shaping your thinking, feeling, evaluating, and acting), you won't experience the metaphors as very influential. But that feeling is hiding a fundamental reality of faith: **the metaphors that shape how you live and how you believe frame and filter your relationship with Jesus.**

As unlikely as it may seem, the conceptual metaphors that frame your faith experience give rise to the uncritical assumptions you make all the time about what it means "to believe," and what that belief should look like in real life. Even when you take time to notice the metaphors you use for faith and life, these filters won't *feel* very important to how you make decisions or what you think you are doing as you follow Jesus. But your feelings are lying to you.

In reality, those filters are critically important: **you understand your faith and live out your life in ways that are consistent with the situational logic of the metaphors you use to frame your experience.**

And that's a good thing! The fact that God chooses *human words* to deliver *the divine Word* also means that the Almighty intentionally chooses to use metaphor to shape you and your life of faith. As my own great-uncle once wrote:

> When words are used, metaphor is inevitable. I hasten to add that this outcome is not at all unfortunate. It is a cause for rejoicing. Our language is the richer for it. Metaphor helps rather than hinders communication. In brief, metaphor is a necessary good.[4]

Draining all the water from the pond is not a viable option for the fish. Just as fish need water to live, we need metaphors to filter and frame our experience and our faith. But what happens when the filters no longer give life?

---

[4] *Preaching the Creative Gospel Creatively* (1983) by Francis Rossow.

Changing the Filter

More and more, the way we typically imagine (and therefore live out) what it means to be a follower of Jesus in the Western Church in the opening act of the twenty-first century seems to miss some of the most important and most joyful aspects of biblical faith. Maybe the water we're swimming in has gotten polluted over time; maybe we need to check the filter.

Dealing with any specific default decision, bad behavior, scriptural misinterpretation, or theological misapplication is only treating the symptoms. **We need a way to diagnose our defaults. We need to *rethink* how we think.**

The goal is to develop habits and skills that allow us to notice and evaluate the water we swim in, to measure the temperature and check the pH balance. We need to know when murky water is hiding uncritical assumptions that hinder faith. We need to know when to swim against the stream. We need a healthy aquatic ecosystem that nurtures and promotes life and health. And we need to know when to change the filter.

Like an ecosystem, the metaphors we use to imagine, understand, and live out our faith form a living network of related ideas. You can't "fix" a system with one silver bullet solution; at the same time, if you affect any part of the system, you also affect the whole. Making one small change in the way you filter faith and following will make other changes more obvious, natural, and even necessary.

If you develop eyes to see the water you are swimming in, you will be able to affect the health of your ecosystem, one metaphor at a time.

Taking a critical look at our uncritical assumptions will probably *feel* like challenging answers that are *obvious*, outcomes that are *natural*, dividing lines that are *clear*, and goals that are *unquestionable*, at least at first.

You might even feel an urge to *protect* the ways we have "always" thought about discipleship. That defense mechanism is natural. An urge to defend the status quo is one side effect of having a filter hard-wired into your imagination: **the filter itself appears natural and obvious in ways that make it difficult to notice, much less change.**

Think about it: what could possibly be *wrong* with "making disciples" or "outreach" or "passing down the faith," right? These kinds of phrases *define what it means to follow Jesus* in our culture.

And because the metaphors behind our common ways of thinking and talking about the life of faith *predetermine how we imagine and experience faith and life*, these filters are powerful, formative, and hidden from view.

The Joy of Getting Back to Jesus

Fish seem to get on just fine without ever thinking about water. So why should I rethink the way I think? My uncritical assumptions are functioning just fine!

That knee jerk reaction isn't completely wrong. Actually, the typical frames we use to understand and live out our Christian faith have indeed *worked just fine* for the age and culture we have most recently been swimming in (for the last few generations at least). That's one reason these frames have become entrenched and almost invisible: over time, those filters have gotten some pretty good results!

But more recently, with the rise of a post-church culture and the decline of Christian influence in general, we have begun to sense that something just isn't working right when it comes to shaping the faith and life of those who would follow Jesus. Our Christian imagination is glitching in several significant ways, and the way we *mis*imagine being the Church has wide-ranging implications.

The solution is neither so simple it will be fast and easy, nor so impossible we don't know where to begin.

If you want to create a healthy, vibrant, and life-giving ecosystem of faith, check your water. Uncover the frames and filters that shape your uncritical assumptions. Notice when your imagination is guided (or misguided) by the most common ways you talk about and experience the life of faith. Then check those frames and filters against the way Jesus imagines what it means to be Church, what it means to disciple, what it means to be called and to follow.

That challenging work of critical self-reflection is necessary if we are going to rethink the way we think about (and live out) being fallen-but-forgiven people in a good-but-fallen world that is already-but-not-yet restored.

Changing a water filter isn't supposed to add something completely new to an aquatic ecosystem; changing the filter simply gets the ecosystem back working the way it's supposed to. In the same way, changing the filters we use for faith means **reimagining discipleship in ways that aren't *foreign*, but actually *more faithful*, to how the Bible has imagined following Jesus all along.** We aren't adding something to the water source; we're checking to make sure the water isn't getting polluted along the way.

As we evaluate our own filters, we'll discover that a more biblical way of imagining following Jesus is not only more faithful, it's also more beautiful; and quite frankly, much more fun. There is joy in getting back to what Jesus had in mind all along when he told the first disciples, "Follow me!" and sent them out to disciple the nations.

. . .

Summary of Chapter 2: Fish Discover Water Last

The things we take for granted are really hard to evaluate because they are so hard to notice in the first place. (That's why "fish discover water last.") Experiments in metaphor and thought show: (1) that the way we frame any situation changes how we experience it and make decisions about it; and (2) that the frame or metaphor itself will not feel very important. It seems somewhat counterintuitive that the frames (or metaphors) we use to imagine (or filter) Christian faith are important; in reality, those dynamics shape our uncritical assumptions—and therefore how we think, feel, make decisions, and live out our faith. If we uncover *what goes without saying*, we can get back to a more biblical (and more beautiful) way of imagining our life with Jesus and relationships with other people.

For Further Reflection

Share a personal story about a time when your uncritical assumptions led to some conclusions or actions that didn't turn out the way you expected.

Even noticing our default modes of thinking can be a challenge. Did this chapter resonate with you? Did you feel a little defensive? Did it seem insightful, or confusing? What challenge or hope do you see as a result of reading?

Brainstorm some common vocabulary we typically use in the Church for faith in Jesus and living out our Christian life:

Can you find any filters hiding behind those words or phrases that frame how we experience or live out our faith? What metaphors do Christians live by? Check the Table of Contents: did any of your insights make the list?

Chapter 3

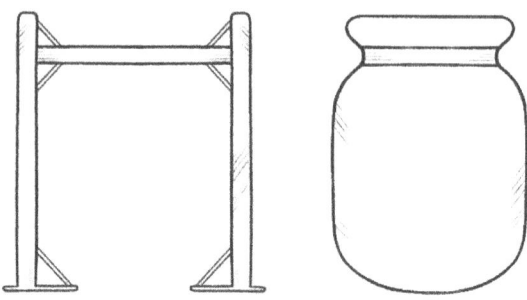

High Bar or Clay Jar?
Something More than "Trying to Be like Jesus"

Our Default Setting: We typically imagine Jesus as the gold standard for faith and life. We naturally set a high bar and work hard to emulate Jesus in what we do. We value being active, doing more, and being in control. We judge ourselves based on the perceived distance from the ideal (Jesus) and on our progress toward the ideal (at least, compared to others around us).

Some Good Reasons for Our Default: Many of our most common experiences tell us control, activity, and having more are all *good* (and *up*). We are encouraged to have high standards and to set high goals and then go after them. Jesus himself says he is leaving an example for us to follow.

Some Unintended Consequences: Individuals are expected to take control of their own active faith development, with Jesus as their goal or standard. When this self-propelled effort falters, individuals either give up trying to emulate Jesus, or justify their efforts on a sliding scale (*at least I am better than the person next to me*). Setting up Jesus as the ideal leads to spiritual bootstrapping and the constant burden of doing more and doing better.

Something More: If you want to shift from a High Bar default to Clay Jar thinking, reimagine the direction of discipleship. Don't set Jesus *up* as a high bar standard of faith and life. Instead, trust the promise that the Spirit comes *down* to meet you, right where you are. You are not in charge of your own faith journey. Like clay being shaped by the potter, you are in the process of being shaped by the Spirit to be more like Jesus.

• • •

Good is Up

I vividly remember watching my daughter compete in the high jump at a middle school track meet. Imagine the scene: the young athlete prepares herself with a few deep breaths as she rocks back and forth in her studs. Suddenly, with a burst of speed, she launches herself at the pit.

Her path angles slightly; she steps just so. Then comes the critical moment: she explodes upward, turning mid-air, arching her back and kicking her feet to clear the crossbar. But she grazes the fiberglass pole just a hair, and, as the athlete slams into the royal blue landing mat, the neon-yellow crossbar seems to ripple for a moment, then clatters to the ground.

Rolling off the thick mat, the high jumper grimaces, but quickly jogs over to her coach for a brief word of correction and encouragement.

Eyes tight and chin set, she gets back in line. Two more faults and she will be eliminated. Clear this height, and she will advance to the finals: the judges will dismiss the disqualified, raise the bar, and start the process over again. With an air of determination, the athlete begins her pre-jump routine...

That high jump exemplifies a dynamic we tend to live by, often unawares. We naturally *reach* for our goal, feel compelled to set *high* standards, or get motivated to *raise* expectations. And when we imagine possibilities, evaluate outcomes, or experience our own actions in terms of *elevating* our performance, or being *up* for the challenge, or *raising* the bar, we are living our lives in terms of an axiom so pervasive, it is all but invisible.

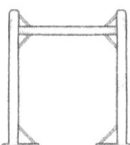

We learn this truism experientially from our interaction with the physical world around us, and it shapes not only our language, but our logic, emotions, and experience, as well. **We *just know* that, for all normal, everyday purposes, anything *good* is probably *up*.**

Orientational Metaphors We Live By

Do you know what it's like to need a pick-me-*up* to *raise* your spirits? Have you ever felt *ten feet tall*? Do you ever *jump* for joy, give your friend a *high* five, or *lift* your hands in victory or praise? If so, your common, everyday, normal physical and emotional experience is telling you that anything *happy* can be equated with the direction *up*.

Conversely, if you know what it means to *fall* into a *depression*, feel *low*, *crash* after a high, get *down* on yourself, or *hang* your head in grief and shame, then everything *sad* will align with the opposite direction: *down*.

In your normal life, you wake *up*, and get *up*, and sober *up*. But you can also *fall* asleep, *sink* into your dreams, or come *under* the influence. In your typical experience, *conscious* is *up*, and *unconscious* is *down* (though you may never have consciously thought of it that way before).

Even concepts like *authority* or *control* are usually experienced as *up*: the orders came from the *top*; she's *head* of the department; he is my *superior*; I'm *climbing* the corporate ladder. Naturally, then, the opposite situation (being *subject to authority*) will be *down*: he is *under* my control; she has you *under* her thumb; he *fell* from a position of power; she got knocked *down* a few rungs.[1]

The notion that Good is fundamentally Up (and Down is Bad) belongs to a special category of "orientational" or "spatialization" metaphors. (You probably don't need to know the jargon, but we will run into more of these later on. In this case, the technical terms are also fairly descriptive.)

---

[1] These "orientational metaphors" are all noted by George Lakoff and Mark Johnson in *Metaphors We Live By*, University of Chicago Press (reprint ed., 2003). The lists of supporting utterances, however, are my own (though I did peek at their list, too).

You wouldn't commonly say the sentence: "Good is up." But orientational metaphors like Good is Up, or Happy is Up, or Control is Up, all belong to the vocabulary of our everyday experience. In fact, all kinds of ordinary, run-of-the-mill expressions make use of our natural experience of physical space. Spatialization metaphors are everywhere![2]

But spatialization metaphors don't merely *shape the way we talk*. Even more, they actually *shape the way we perceive and evaluate ourselves and others*. To complicate things further, the influence of these metaphors seems so obvious and natural, most of the time we aren't even aware of it!

Without trying to (or meaning to) we end up experiencing the Christian life as a continuum from Down to Up, with Jesus at the top, and me trying my best to be *active* and *in control*, to strive harder to be *more* (even if it's more humble or more sacrificial) so I can live *up* to good, Christian expectations. On that continuum, it's easy for discipleship to focus almost exclusively on my own, personal effort: as a believer, my job is to do more and to do better, to try harder and get higher.

As soon as you have a continuum, you also have the means to evaluate yourself and other people. Set whatever kind of bar you like—income, happiness, moral behavior, proficiency—and you automatically become a competitive high jumper. The bar tells you how well you are doing, but also (and here's the kicker) how well you are doing *compared to everyone else*.

You didn't get the raise you deserved, but some people didn't get any pay increase at all; you aren't doing as well as you wanted, but *at least you are doing better than some other people* measured by the same bar.

You may not have reached your goals for personal finance or personal fitness or personal relationships, but you know people who are backsliding or whose careers are in free fall. *At least you aren't like them...*

---

[2] Using all caps, as in "GOOD is UP," was a fairly standard convention early on in Cognitive Linguistics to signify a "conceptual metaphor" (the structure of our thought and experience) as distinct from a linguistic expression (the words we say). But the ALL CAPS can feel like we are SHOUTING OUR METAPHORS all over the place, so I will stick with another accepted convention to label conceptual metaphors like Good is Up.

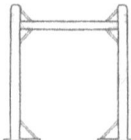

Things are really looking up for you; but the neighbors just bought a new car, and put in a new pool, and then today they recycled the empty cardboard box for the very same ultra-high-def TV you have been coveting since last Christmas. All of a sudden, your Up doesn't seem quite as high by comparison. You might even feel a bit like a failure, even though life is good.

Set any kind of bar as high as you like, and you will always find people on the Up/Down continuum who are higher than you; and some others who are lower (and falling fast). **When you compare yourself and your progress to other people on the sliding scale of Up to Down, you will always have reason to feel good about yourself (compared to some people), *and* bad about yourself (compared to others).**

Feelings of pride, envy, accomplishment, self-justification, frustration, fear of failure, confidence, exhaustion, and exhilaration (to name a few) all belong to a domain of Competition where your performance is compared to others relative to a standard. Those emotions also naturally and automatically carry over to any area of life where you can use a scale of Up and Down to judge yourself compared to others.

You don't *decide* to gloat, or feel like life is unfair, or experience less income as failure: you just *do*. It seems obvious and natural. It goes without saying.

And when that kind of Up/Down evaluation (and competition) gets read into the Bible and applied to the life of the Church, discipleship becomes a striving *upward*, toward a bar you can never quite reach. (But at least you are doing better than that one guy in the next pew...)

I am convinced that Jesus wants something more for us than that.

Spatialization Metaphors across Cultures

When it comes to basic dichotomies like Up/Down or In/Out, we should *expect* the Bible to utilize some of the same spatialization metaphors we do. Although the panoply of biblical authors are writing in cultures, languages, and historical settings vastly separated from us (and often from each other), they are also writing as human beings in human bodies, communicating by human means to other human beings (even when divinely inspired).

Diverse human bodies relate to the physical world around us in some fundamentally similar ways. Even across cultural and language barriers, **we can therefore anticipate some similarities in assumptions and expectations when metaphors are grounded in our physical interaction with the world.**[3]

Whether you are living as a slave in Ancient Egypt, a government official in Ancient Babylon, a tax collector in first century Palestine, or web designer in contemporary America, your human body experiences the world in strikingly similar ways. By and large, you will naturally sleep lying Down, get Up to be more active, and learn from experience that having More of a good thing is better than not having enough.

This common human experience facilitates communication across time and culture. But the focus of this chapter is not to demonstrate how our common conceptual metaphors *help us understand* the Bible (which they do). It's not even to call out all the possible ways our cultural variation of the Up/Down continuum *gets the biblical text wrong* (which it can).

Instead, this chapter is zoomed in on how a highly competitive, pull-yourself-*up*-by-your-bootstraps kind of culture leads to an experience of following Jesus that requires more and more effort from the individual. **By setting *Jesus* as the bar every disciple is trying to reach, we are in danger of reversing the direction of sanctification (as well as salvation) and missing all the best parts of spiritual growth and formation.**

Setting the Bar at Jesus

It has to be said: the Bible does indeed talk about Jesus as a kind of example. Jesus himself can say, "I have set you *an example* that you should do as I have done for you;" or even, "Very truly I tell you, whoever believes in me will do the works I have been doing, and they will do even greater things than these..." (John 13:15; 14:12, NIV).

Because Good is Up on the continuum, Even Better is Even Higher.

---

[3] See Zoltán Kövecses, *Metaphor in Culture: Universality and Variation*, Cambridge University Press, 2006. He does a great job of exploring how and why we see similarities and differences in common conceptual metaphors across language groups and individuals.

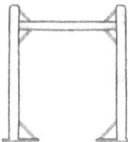

So it's natural for us to understand the Jesus example as the gold standard, the high bar which we are supposed to reach, and even surpass.

We don't think about it. We don't *have to* think about it. We *just know* that Jesus is the measuring stick, and our job is to get *up* to that level of holiness in action. So we strap on our sweatbands and WWJD bracelets, eye that distant fiberglass pole a little askance, and begin our warm up routine. Time to take another run at clearing the bar!

As you might expect, Christian living counts as one of those unique circumstances where *less* is sometimes *more*. (The "example" Jesus set in John 13, after all, was leaving his place of honor to get down on his knees and wash the disciples' feet.)

Christian virtues like humility, or repentance, or dependence often involve a kind of upside-down thinking—lose yourself, die to yourself, give it all away, in order to find yourself, live a new life, and gain the Kingdom. But even when Jesus "sets the bar" at kneeling *down* with a dirty towel, **we experience, reason, and feel like that bar is Up; in fact, that bar can feel unachievably high.** [4]

Which, if we are operating in a competition mode, doesn't really seem *fair*. We can try really hard to be like Jesus, but it's clearly not a level playing field.

Jesus has distinct advantages when it comes to leading a good and moral life (like *being God*, for instance). How am I supposed to live *up* to that?

Sometimes we soften the expectation to make it more palatable: just do your best ... and maybe a little better than the person next to you (as if God were grading on a curve, and we all get participation trophies in the end).

---

[4] You can find exceptions to any general rule, in language as well as in life. In some instances, you can have More of a bad thing, in which case Good is *not* Up: inflation is *rising*; homelessness is *up*; the crime rate is at an all-time *high*. In these cases, More is Up takes precedence over Good is Up in our conceptual and linguistic system. Those kinds of special cases are a normal deviation from the accepted standard: even though Good is Up, and More is Up, More can, in the right circumstance, also be Bad.

Look closer, and you'll find another special set of circumstances: if Less of something is Good, then Less can be Up (because Good is Up). So you could say, "I lost ten pounds and finally *reached* my weight goal." (Although your weight was going down, the goal is something Up for which you reach.) Or you could aspire to one day *attain the level* of organization evidenced by Marie Kondo (which would definitely mean less stuff, not more). In special circumstances—in this case, whenever you could say, "Less is more,"—the general rule can be broken. Less can be Good, and even Up.

Sometimes we point to Jesus and his solidarity with us as if that were a comfort. I have recently heard multiple times from the pulpit some version of "Jesus won't ask you to do anything he hasn't done first." Which is great. Except, how am *I* supposed to do what *Jesus* did, even if he did it first? The bar set by the perfect Son of God still feels awfully high...

Sometimes, in our contemporary Church culture, we set that bar as high as we reasonably can and, like cheerleaders on the sideline, encourage people to *give it all they've got*. More than one "discipleship method" developed in the last 30 years revolves around the basic idea: "Here's what Jesus has done for you; now what are *you* going to do about it?"

We can't hardly help ourselves. We experience Christian living as an Up/Down continuum. Jesus is the high bar, and I end up trying my *active* best to be *in control*, to do *more* and do *better*, so I can be like Jesus and someday live Up to his example.

The specifics may be subject to personal and local variation, but in general, **our own effort and activity will seem like the driving force that propels upward movement toward a goal.** In a competitive culture that values personal motivation and individual achievement, the answer feels unavoidable: if you only work harder, run faster, and jump higher, you will eventually clear the bar.

Then you are expected to raise the bar a little higher and do it all again. It's time to pull yourself up by your spiritual bootstraps and get to work!

Noticing Assumptions of Up and Down

Because we *just know* that Good is Up, Active is Up, More is Up, and Control is Up, we will naturally *value* being active, doing more, having more, and being in control. Communities of believers will tend to prioritize (and therefore *measure*) the kinds of things that fit with our basic experience that Good is Up, because the Up/Down continuum typically defines worth and value for us.

Congregations naturally value (and measure) *active* membership and *increasing* attendance numbers because Active is Up and More is Up.

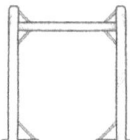

A loss of Christian influence in the public sphere seems like an obvious ecclesial crisis in part because Control is Up, and losing control means *shrinking* influence, a *decline* in membership, and a *lower* status in our culture (all obviously and intuitively Down, and therefore Bad).

If membership is *up*, and giving is *up*, and active volunteerism is *up*, we obviously feel pretty good about the trajectory of our local church; if those things are *down*, we know without further reflection that our congregation is in *decline*.

If we want more members or more spiritual growth, **we naturally find solutions that fit the way we have framed the problem in the first place.** We add *more* church activities and church programs. We encourage people to *more* social activism or *more* prayer or *more* service in the community. We make sure we *increase* opportunities for people to do more and do better, because Active is Up, and More is Up, and Good is Up.

I am not suggesting these options or inferences are wrong out of hand, or proposing that smaller churches are better, or hoping for lower standards, decreased giving, or declining cultural influence. I simply want to notice that **most of the inferences we make about what is good or bad** when it comes to things like worship attendance, giving, membership, social influence, budgets, volunteerism, and personal piety **seem so obvious and natural that they go without saying, and therefore, without any conscious thought or reflection.**

What we think, how we feel, the things we count as progress, what we hope for and pray for and strive for, personally and institutionally, all tend to operate on a scale of Up and Down, Good and Bad.

That cultural understanding shapes not only our diagnosis of the problem, it makes some solutions seem obvious and natural, while other possibilities are deemphasized or even hidden completely from view.[5] **As long as High Bar thinking is the only way we process the challenges of "trying to be like Jesus," we will only find answers that involve a personal effort to do more, try harder, and get better (or at least, better than *some* people we could mention).**

---

[5] Lakoff and Johnson talk about metaphor's power to highlight and hide in Chapter 3 of *Metaphors We Live By*.

While an Up/Down scale *feels* natural, obvious, and inevitable—as if it were *just part of the way the world works*—there is no divine mandate to view the world that way. Once we notice the assumptions that go without saying, we can go back to Scripture and wonder about the Jesus example, or the seemingly obvious movement Up toward more and better Christian living.

We can try to read the Bible on its own terms, rather than imposing an Up vs Down continuum on every aspect of biblical theology. We can try to imagine other ways of framing the Christian life besides *striving upward*, and wonder what alternatives might look like, for Christian communities as well as individual followers.

We won't reject Good is Up robotically; but we will try to be more and more aware of the pervasive power of the assumption that *Good is always Up*. It's all too easy for that fundamental mindset to go unnoticed, in part because that way of framing the world is so natural and automatic for us.

We're fish discovering water. It isn't easy. But it can be beautiful. And maybe even fun.

Salvation is Down

While we tend to experience Good as Up, **the biblical witness seems to see salvation as a *coming down*.** God *comes down* to rescue a people from Egypt (Exodus 3:8). God *comes down* to cut covenant with that redeemed people at Sinai (Exodus 19:11). The prophet's plea for salvation is that Yahweh would "rend the heavens and *come down*" (Isaiah 64:1).

Jesus is the living bread that *comes down* from heaven to give life to the world (John 6:33). On the Last Day, the Lord himself will *come down* (1 Thessalonians 4:16). Likewise, the New Jerusalem will *come down* out of heaven from God (Revelation 21:10).

Even when the Bible does contrast heaven (Up) with earth (Down)—"Their minds are set on earthly things. But our citizenship is in heaven..."—*Salvation* is still not Up, but remains Down—"... and it is *from there* that we are expecting a Savior, the Lord Jesus Christ" (Philippians 3:19-20).

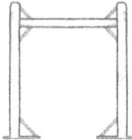

As finite human beings, we can't actually get all the way *Up* to God on our own; the people at Babel tried, building a tower *up* to the heavens. And, ironically, God has to come all the way *down* just to see what those humans are up to (Genesis 11:3-5).

You might go Up the mountain to meet with God—at Sinai or Zion or even the Mount of Transfiguration—but that's only because that mountain is the place where God chooses to come Down and dwell with people—in the Tabernacle, the Temple, and the person of Jesus.

God's saving action is characterized not merely as a lifting *up* of those who are low, but as God coming *down* to be with and for the lowly.

Jesus himself says he is an example, but not an example "up there" for us to reach; not a high bar or gold standard for us to achieve. Jesus lowers himself all the way to our level, and then lowers himself even further. In the actions of a common household slave, washing the disciples' feet, Jesus says he has set an example, to do as he has done (John 13:12-15) and love as he loves (John 13:34-35).

Salvation is Down.

And if Salvation is Down, we might begin to suspect that Discipleship is Down, as well. But if Discipleship is *Down*, **that changes the entire trajectory and orientation of faith development.** Your job is no longer to work hard to attain the higher level of holy living evidenced by Jesus. If Discipleship is Down, you aren't even the primary actor when it comes to being more like Jesus because *you* aren't the one who comes *down*.

The Spirit Who Comes Down

It's easy to see *Jesus* as the primary actor in *salvation*; he is, after all, the one who comes down from heaven and does all the important salvation stuff. But when it comes to sanctification, or discipleship, or Christian living, it often feels like *I* am the primary actor, trying my best to do more and do better. We're back to the "Here's what Jesus has done for you; now what are you going to do about it?" paradigm of discipleship.

An approach to discipleship that paints *me* as the primary actor resonates with a culture where Good is Up, and Active is Up, and Control is Up. But such an approach entirely misses the work of the Spirit, not only in the life of the believer, but in the life and ministry of Jesus.

What Jesus comes *Down* to do for you, he does in the power of the Holy Spirit. The Spirit descends (comes down) and rests on Jesus as his baptism (Matthew 3). The Spirit leads (or drives) Jesus out into the wilderness to be tempted by the devil (Matthew 4). Jesus returns from that struggle and begins his ministry in the power of the Spirit (Luke 4). Jesus, as the Messiah or "Anointed One," is by definition and calling the "Anointed-with-the-Spirit One," who completes his mission as the one who receives, bears, and pours out the Holy Spirit.[6]

Just as the Spirit came down to hover over the waters of creation, and came down to alight on Jesus in the waters of his baptism, so the Spirit still descends and empowers and takes up residence in all those who are baptized into the End Times death and Renewed Creation resurrection of the Messiah (Romans 6).

As the Spirit came down and shook the house and filled the disciples on Pentecost (Acts 2), so the Spirit still comes down and fills both individuals and the Church, so that we—personally and corporately—become a living Temple, a place where God dwells by the power of the Spirit (Ephesians 2); not just Up there in heaven, but Down here, where we need God's presence most.

We tend to reason about and experience salvation as a raising Up; but prior and more fundamental to the act of raising Up, Jesus comes Down.

In a similar way, we tend to reason about and experience sanctification and faith development as a kind of progress Up. But prior and more fundamental to the act of spiritual growth, the Spirit comes Down.

The Spirit comes down and rests on Jesus, so that everything the Anointed One does for you, he does in the power of the Spirit.

---

[6] For a more detailed account of the Spirit's work in the life of Jesus and, consequently, in the life of the believer, see *Sculptor Spirit: Models of Sanctification from Spirit Christology*, Leopoldo A. Sánchez M.

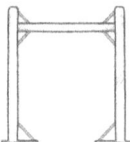

Then Jesus sends the Spirit to come down and rest on you, so that everything Jesus is *for* you, the Spirit now shapes *in* you.

Discipleship doesn't work like a pole vault; your job is not to train harder and do better so you can reach higher. Discipleship is more like a clay vase; the Spirit shapes you to look more and more like Jesus, bit by bit, over time.

Like the clay, **you are intimately involved in the process.** But, also like the clay, **you aren't the one in control.**[7]

Change your default setting from High Bar to Clay Jar, and what you believe, think, hope for, and pray for in spiritual formation will change. Instead of striving to get Up, you will start looking for the Spirit to come Down.

And that's when the real adventure begins...

Follow Me, and I Will Shape You

Discipleship is more about the passive act of *being shaped* than a self-initiated activity to move yourself up the moral ladder. Like a sculptor with marble or a potter with clay, the Spirit is chiseling away at your heart and molding your life.

But the divine artist isn't shaping you at random. Just as the sculptor or potter has a model or design in mind, the Spirit shapes you with a purpose. When the Spirit shapes you, the Spirit has Jesus in mind. While the clay may feel completely out of control, confused, spinning frantically, unbalanced, and unable to see the big picture, the Potter has the situation well in hand.

Maybe Jesus is a *model* after all; not a model athlete for us to reach up and emulate, but **an artist's model for the Spirit to come down and shape in us.** And when the work is most intense for the clay, the eyes of the Potter are focused most intently on the work, molding with great patience, skill, and care.

---

[7] Elsewhere, I have used Philippians 2:12-13 (**Work out your salvation** with fear and trembling, for it is **God who works in you,** both to will and to do) to talk about our active engagement in a process we do not control. It's kind of like whitewater kayaking: you aren't in charge of your progress or destination; the river is. At the same time, you are strapped in, paddling furiously, and sopping wet. Discipleship is like that. See *Delight! Discipleship as the Adventure of Loving and Being Loved* (2020), chapter 10, God's Work Shapes Your Adventure.

How far do we want to extend the sculpting metaphor? In our individualistic culture, it seems obvious and natural that the individual sculpture correlates to the individual person; we naturally think of faith formation as the formation of my, personal, individual faith. But the Bible is probably more likely to imagine us being formed and shaped, and even useful and beautiful, *in community,* so we'll want to avoid a natural isolationism that could flow from the sculptor lens.

Here's another way we might naturally get the potter image wrong: in a culture that values *usefulness* and *end products,* it's natural and obvious to place more value on the clay once it is finished and being used. I mean, you would pay more for a skilled potter's end product than for some clay that's only half-formed, right?

But in the mystery of Already and Not Yet that characterizes the lives of those who live by faith and not by sight, you are already valued and cherished and beloved *even though you are still in the process of being shaped.*

You aren't trying to get better so you can achieve more and maybe get God to love you a little better or give you what you want. Discipleship isn't exactly about *improvement;* and discipleship is never about *self-*improvement.

Your value is not tied up in how much you improve, or how high you reach, or even how hard you try. But your value is also not tied up in your usefulness to other people or how much you impact the lives of other. There is no guarantee that you will see your own growth (though you often will) and no guarantee that you will see how useful and helpful you are to others (though, by and large, all things being equal, in the normal course of being shaped into Christlikeness, you will see an impact on the people around you).

In other words, the Up/Down continuum we so naturally use to evaluate ourselves and our experience can creep back into our thinking about spiritual formation without us even being aware of it.

If you evaluate your discipleship in terms of *personal effort* or *personal experience* or *personal improvement,* you will naturally see More as Up, and Control as Up, and Better as Up. If you evaluate your own spiritual formation in terms of how *much impact you have on others,* you will tend to use the same grading scale: More is Up, and Control is Up, and Better is Up.

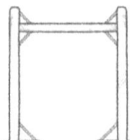

Noticing that we are being conformed to the image of Christ *for the sake of others* can help relieve an inherent self-centeredness.[8] But that focus can also emphasize our own value or activity (even if it is value to others).

Which doesn't mean you won't experience change and blessing and joy and growth (in yourself and in your service to others) as the Spirit continues to shape Jesus in you! It's just that you walk by faith and not by sight. You won't always see or understand what the Potter is doing. It won't *always* feel like you are making progress or being more of a blessing to others.

As clay spun on the wheel and touched by the Spirit's shaping hands, you are not in control of the process.

You don't even get to decide how to evaluate the process.

You can't always see what the Potter is doing, so you trust, beyond what you can see, that the Spirit is shaping Jesus in you.

You will likely have moments of great joy as you glimpse how much you have changed or how your spiritual formation has actually been used by God to help other people. And sometimes, you won't see that clearly at all.

God doesn't delight in you more when you start to look more like Jesus. God doesn't delight in you more because you are more useful. But God does delight in shaping you; and, when and where it pleases God, and to God's glory, you get to see how God is using you for the sake of others.

That process begins before you know it is happening, and often takes place without your conscious awareness. *Being shaped* is always an integral part of the job description of following Jesus, even when you can't see it. When Jesus calls his disciples, he calls them to an ongoing adventure that invites their hearts, lives, understanding, will, self-evaluation, personal history, and plans for the future to be subject to a beautiful design, not their own.

"Come, follow me," Jesus says, "And I will shape you ..." (Mark 1). At that part of the story, Jesus is specifically saying that he will take these specific

---

[8] M. Robert Mulholland's definition for "spiritual formation" is one I think applies to what we have been calling "discipleship." In his book, *Invitation to a Journey*, Mulholland says spiritual formation (discipleship) is "the process of being conformed to the image of Christ for the sake of others."

fishermen and transform them, over time, into the kind of people who "fish" for other people. "I will make you to be fishers of men."

But that "make you" verb is a "shape you, mold you, form you" verb. It's the same vocabulary a potter would use for the clay.

"Follow me, and I will *sculpt* you."

That promise is at the heart of the call to discipleship. Whether you are a professional fisherman or not, the call to follow Jesus is a call to come and be shaped and molded, sculpted and formed, into something new, and beautiful, and more full of life than you could possibly imagine.

Just like the New Creation is neither a simple do-over nor something completely different, the New Creation life being shaped in you already now, ahead of time, is **a total transformation that, in some mysterious way, also makes you *more you*, even as you become more like Christ.**[9]

Dependence is Down

Our natural instincts tell us: Active is Up, More is Up, Control is Up, and Good is Up. We know there are exceptions to the rules of those basic orientational metaphors, but without clear context or conscious effort, those spatialization metaphors lead us to think, act, feel, and believe as if *we* are Down, and it is *our job* (with a little help) to get Up and do Better.

So when we hear Jesus say things like:

> I have given you **an example**, that you also should do **just as I have done**.
>
> John 13:15 (ESV)

Or:

> A new commandment I give to you, that you love one another: **just as I have loved you**, you also are to love one another.
>
> John 13:34 (ESV)

---

[9] See the discussion of "Testing the Limits" of the Potter and Clay metaphor in *Preaching Metaphor: How to Shape Sermons that Shape People* by Justin Rossow (2019).

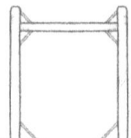

Or even:

> Truly, truly, I say to you, whoever believes in me will also do the works that I do; and **greater works than these** will he do, because I am going to the Father.
>
> John 14:12 (ESV)

—when we hear Jesus say things like that, it is most natural for us to locate Jesus Up on a continuum, and to locate ourselves Down. And if I am Down and Jesus is Up, then it seems obvious and natural that my job is to work harder and do more to get better at living out my faith.

The call to follow gets translated into a call to take Control, be Active, and do More so you can reach Up to the Good Jesus has done. Apparently, you have to do even More and get even Higher than the bar set by Jesus; Jesus says we have to do *even greater works than these*.

I imagine that's not exactly how most of us would articulate our attitude toward discipleship; but I also suspect that our emotions, logic, evaluation of ourselves (and of others), our assumptions about what to do next and what counts as progress or failure, **all secretly hinge on an assumption that goes without saying: Good is Up, and we are Down, and we had better get going.**

Such an obvious and natural understanding of the text misses some of the most important dynamics of what Jesus is actually saying, and misconstrues what Jesus is actually inviting us into.

Right after Jesus gives his followers an example, Jesus clarifies:

> Truly, truly, I say to you, **whoever receives the one I send receives me,** and whoever receives me **receives the one who sent me.**
>
> John 13:20 (ESV)

Immediately before Jesus says his followers will do "even greater things than these" (John 14:12), he says:

> Do you not believe that **I am in the Father** and the Father is in me? The words that I say to you **I do not speak on my own authority**, but the **Father who dwells in me does his works.** Believe me that **I am in the Father** and the Father is in me...
>
> John 14:10-11 (ESV)

It's not just *the works* you are called to emulate; it's *the way of working*. Jesus, who has received the Spirit and claims that the Father is in him—that the Father is the one doing the work in and through him (!)—goes on to invite his disciples into that same kind of intimacy with the Spirit and the Father:

> I will ask the Father, and **he will give you another Helper, to be with you forever, even the Spirit of truth,** whom the world cannot receive, because it neither sees him nor knows him. You know him, for **he dwells with you and will be in you.** I will not leave you as orphans; **I will come to you** ...
>
> In that day you will know that **I am in my Father,** and **you in me,** and **I in you** ... If anyone loves me, he will keep my word, and my Father will love him, and **we will come to him** and **make our home** with him.
>
> John 14:16-18, 20, 23 (ESV)

Notice the *direction* and the *location* of the activity that counts as "following Jesus' example" and "doing the works" Jesus did: the Spirit and the Father dwell in Jesus, *Down* where Jesus is, doing their work in and through Jesus. Jesus is going away, but he will send the Spirit *Down* to his disciples, so that Jesus himself can be *Down* with them and in them.

Jesus lives out an intimate dependence on the Father and the Spirit; and then makes a way for you to enter into that same intimate dependence. You—*you!*—are now brought into a relationship with the Almighty God that is located Down; down here; *down where you already are.*

The intimacy of the Trinity is extended, by grace, to include the individual believer as well as the Church.[10]

It's no wonder that John 13 (the Footwashing and New Command) and John 14 (the Promise of the Spirit) are followed immediately by John 15 (the Vine and the Branches). The message is the same: active engagement only comes through ongoing, intimate dependence.

---

[10] In this section, Jesus is going back and forth between singular ("the one who") and plural ("y'all"). I take that to correspond to the *personal* and *corporate* nature of faith: we always believe and belong as individuals; and we are also saved as and into a community. For many of the same cultural and contextual dynamics we have noticed in this chapter, it's easy for us to read the Bible as *only,* or *primarily,* about the individual. This footnote is just a friendly reminder to keep the community in your heart and mind. The call to follow is a call into community.

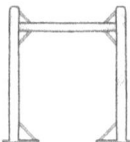

> **Abide in me**, and **I in you**. As the branch cannot bear fruit by itself, unless it **abides in the vine**, neither can you, unless you **abide in me** ...
>
> As the Father has loved me, so have I loved you. **Abide in my love.** If you keep my commandments, you will **abide in my love**, just as I have kept my Father's commandments and **abide in his love**. These things I have spoken to you, that **my joy may be in you**, and that your joy may be full.
>
> John 15:4, 9-11 (ESV)

All that talk of bearing fruit and keeping commands could easily be construed in terms of Active is Up, and Control is Up, and More is Up. In spite of the context, I think we naturally and automatically read our default orientational and spatialization metaphors back into the text. Then John 13-15 becomes about *me*, and about doing my best to work hard and produce more and better fruit.

But that natural and automatic reading gets it backwards! (Or upside down?) Like the rest of the Bible, John 13-15 is not first and foremost about *me*. It's about *Jesus*, who is living out dependence on the Father and the Spirit.

If Active is Up, then Dependence is Down. And Jesus promises that the Spirit will come Down to dwell with believers; that both Jesus and the Father will dwell with them. And then, *in the power of that ongoing abiding presence,* the branches will end up bearing much fruit.

Trying hard to produce more and better fruit makes as much sense as trying to pull yourself out of the quicksand by your own ponytail.[11] You shouldn't expect that to work for you, or for anyone else!

You are indeed *actively* and even *joyfully* engaged, but only because *the Spirit is shaping your joyful desire as well as your action* (see Philippians 2:12-13). You aren't working hard to get yourself Up; the Spirit, who comes Down, is hard at

---

[11] Ironically, the colloquialism "to pull yourself up by your bootstraps" started out as a disparaging description of a ludicrously impossible action; but, according to dictionary.com and uselessetymology.com, that phrase has more recently come to be a simple description of self-reliance and independence. When a computer "boots up" or "reboots," for example, it is getting itself up and running, *bootstrapping* in an independent and self-sufficient way. That, my friends, is indicative of the independent and self-sufficient culture we live in, where it actually seems to make sense to pull yourself up by your own spiritual bootstraps. Steeped in such rugged individualism, why would it ever occur to us to desperately need Jesus?

work in you and through you. The job description for disciples is not: work harder and faster to do more and get better. (What a relief!)

Disciples are the ones who are called to *be shaped*; to *abide,* and therefore to *bear fruit.* Disciples are the ones called to imitate Jesus' dependence on the Father and the Spirit, and in so doing, to know the joy of the intimate indwelling of the Triune God.

Your prayer is not, "Thank you, Jesus! I'll take it from here!"

Thanks be to God, you are the ones invited to pray, "Come, Holy Spirit, and shape Jesus in me!"

. . .

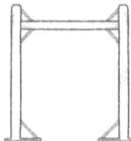

Summary of Chapter 3: High Bar or Clay Jar?

We experience a continuum from Up to Down in our everyday interaction with the physical world around us. The natural and obvious evaluations, conclusions, and expectations inherent in that interaction get carried over into a variety of situations through "spatial" or "orientational" metaphors. These pervasive tools of reasoning, feeling, and evaluating help us understand ourselves and the world around us.

Because Good is Up, and things like being Active, being in Control, having Authority, and having More are also Up, we naturally and without thinking about it value being active, being in control, having authority, and doing more.

When we set the bar for Christian living at Jesus, and then expect people to live up to that standard, the Christian life ultimately becomes full of burden and shame. If I am Down and Jesus is Up, then it seems obvious and natural that my job is to *work harder* and *do more* to *get better* at living out my faith.

Because we use a continuum of Up and Down to evaluate ourselves and others, there will always be people who aren't doing as much or as well as I am. But the fact that *at least I'm better than some people I could mention* is a hollow kind of comfort.

In contrast, the biblical witness locates both salvation and sanctification Down. Jesus comes Down to save; the Spirit comes Down to shape Jesus in you. Jesus lives out intimate dependence on the Spirit and the Father. You as an individual believer, and we together as the Church, are invited into the intimacy of the Trinity, not Up in heaven, but Down here in our ordinary, everyday lives.

Discipleship is not grounded in your effort to do more or get better at reaching the high bar set by Jesus. Discipleship is the process of being shaped by the Spirit to look more and more like Jesus. The divine Potter shapes and uses you, according to divine timing and purpose, to benefit and delight others, even when you can't see it. You become more and more fully yourself as you are shaped to be more and more like Christ.

This Changes Everything

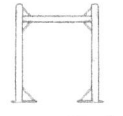

	Setting a High Bar	Potter and Clay
Jesus	The gold standard for your faith and behavior. The example and model you strive to reach.	The sculptor's model and potter's design that the Spirit uses to shape and mold you; what you start to look like in the process.
The Church	A training ground that helps you work hard and get better at reaching the high bar of being like Jesus (and tells you when you fall short and who you are better than).	An artist's studio filled with clay pots in different stages of the process. Unique and beautiful in variety and purpose, for the glory of God and the benefit of others.
The World	People who weigh you down or get in the way of reaching UP to your goal.	People who receive the benefit of the Sculptor's beautiful and useful pots.
The Goal	Live up to the standard of Jesus. Be like Jesus. When you are down in the muck, try harder and do better. (Spiritual bootstrapping.)	Be shaped by the Spirit to look more like Jesus.
My Role	Do more. Try harder. Get better. Judge myself and others based on performance.	Trust the work of the potter even when the process seems confusing to the clay. Be shaped and be formed. Abide in the vine and, as a result, bear fruit.
Key Thinking	Try harder next time!	Come, Holy Spirit, and shape Jesus in me!

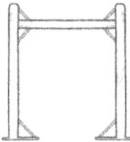

For Further Reflection

Working from within the common paradigm Good is Up, More is Up, Active is Up, and Control is Up, what kinds of things would you expect to *increase* "discipleship" at your congregation? How would you measure success?

Working from within a Discipleship is Down or "abiding produces fruit" mentality, what kinds of things would you expect to *deepen* "discipleship" at your congregation? How would you measure success?

What kinds of things do you (or your congregation) do to increase or measure discipleship?

What benefits or challenges have you experienced?

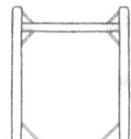

"Here's what Jesus did for you; now what are you going to do about it?" or "Come, Holy Spirit, and shape Jesus in me!" Which of those discipleship mindsets has been modeled for you? How and by whom?

How do you shift toward more dependence on Jesus without making it all about "trying harder" and "doing better" at dependence?

Chapter 4

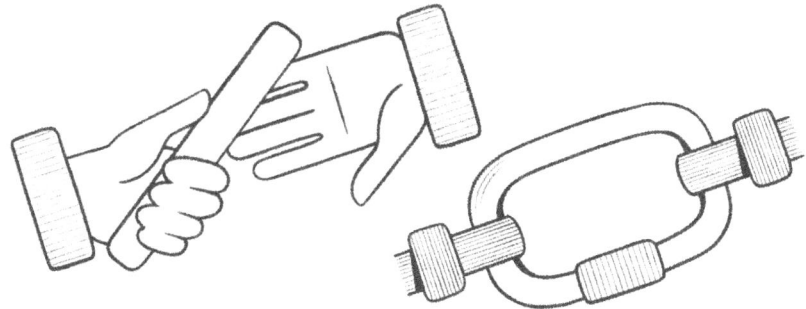

Relay Race or Rope Team?
Something More than "Passing on the Faith"

Our Default Setting: We typically imagine faith as an object that can be passed from one person to another, like passing a torch or passing a baton. We do our part as fast and as independently as we can; then give "the faith" to the next generation and let them run with it. We naturally strive to minimize the time spent in close proximity to others.

Some Good Reasons for Our Default: We know how important it is to instill genuine faith in the next generation. We want our kids and grandkids to know and follow Jesus. Our most natural way of handling ideas or beliefs is in terms we borrow from our interaction with physical objects.

Some Unintended Consequences: Our common identity gets lived out in isolation. Only older and wiser Christians "pass on the faith" to younger, less experienced Christians. Older and wiser Christians are not expected to need any help or support. Younger and less experienced Christians are not expected to offer any help or support until they are older. They are isolated, passive observers until leadership is thrust suddenly on them. If they step out of their lane or drop the baton, the whole team loses.

Something More: To go from a Relay Race dynamic to more of a Rope Team approach to intergenerational discipleship, rethink the way you frame faith relationships. Instead of seeing faith as an object that gets passed down in one direction, with prescribed boundaries and the pressure to get the handoff right, imagine discipleship as a kind of faith expedition. Keep your mountaineering group connected by a safety rope; then expect learning and leadership and mutual support from everyone on the rope as you walk together on the journey.

• • •

Noticing How We Think

It's always hard to notice how you think; it just seems so natural and obvious. In times of crisis, it's even harder to process *how you process.*

If the bad guys are shooting at us and bullets are flying, who has time to think about *why we think* of them as "bad" guys?

When the waves are swamping the boat, who even notices the inherent dynamics of *In* and *Out*? You just bail for all you are worth!

I think something like that may be going on with multi-generational faith formation in the Church. We feel like we are in crisis mode, maybe even under attack, and the boat seems in danger of sinking.

We feel so compelled to do something, *anything*, that it's hard to stop long enough to notice how the *something* we choose to do—even the way we feel about and imagine the crisis, what solutions seem natural (or even possible), what counts as winning or losing, why and how you pray, what we expect and what we ignore—it's hard to stop and notice that **all of that is directly dependent on how we think about faith formation in the first place.**

So it's not easy, but let's try to take half a step back to gain some perspective. Let's process a little more carefully how we process multigenerational faith formation. Let's see if we can quiet the mounting panic long enough to notice where some of that panic may be coming from.

Let's think about how we think.

The Relay Race of Faith

The logic inherent in "passing on the faith" stands out when you put that logic into action. Pretend you could choose five different people from your home congregation who are all at least ten years apart in age. (I have actually done this in several real-life settings, and it can be a lot of fun.) In your imagination, make sure you have someone who is about 10 and someone who is at least 65, with the rest of the people somewhat evenly spaced between.

Now, in your imagination (or with the real people in your Bible study or at your church picnic) run an experiment. The patterns of experience and expectation we use to reason about things like faith formation often start in our bodies, so getting bodies actively engaged helps make the hidden logic behind "passing down the faith" easier to see and evaluate.[1]

For your experiment, set up a relay race with those five different people from your church in their five different life stages. Make sure your relay race has a clear starting block and finish line. Then space the generations out along the track, but in the same lane, so they can compete together as a team.

In your mind's eye, you can give them an actual baton and place them in a clearly defined lane in your local Olympic stadium. When I do this in real life, in a sermon or a workshop, I just have volunteers from different generations spread out around the room and give them an imaginary line to keep them in-bounds. And I don't have a real baton, so I just use an empty paper towel roll.

The runners are ready! The stopwatch is set! The crowd buzzes with expectation and the thrill of competition! On your mark, get set, go!

The octogenarian in the starting position deftly rounds the first curve. He passes the baton (or paper towel roll) to a recently retired business woman, who is anxious to make up for time lost in the transition.

---

[1] The metaphors we live by are often understood intuitively through an automatic and mostly unconscious process called "embodied simulation." Imagining how an experience works in terms of how our bodies interact with the world around us gives us the key to understanding what to expect or how to act when we apply that experience to a new situation. See the discussion of "stamping out racism" in Raymond Gibbs and Teenie Matlock, "Metaphor, Imagination, and Simulation: Psycholinguistic Evidence" in Gibbs, ed., *The Cambridge Handbook of Metaphor and Thought* (161–176), for one example.

She grabs and holds that object, and then quickly passes the baton to a father who recently became an empty-nester.

He then sprints the baton to a young mother who is not only pregnant, but holding a toddler suffering from separation anxiety because Mom stood up and volunteered.[2] (I'm not making that part up; it actually happened that way in real life!)

It almost doesn't seem fair to see that young woman running with her hands full, working hard to cover the distance to our last athlete. But Mom is a real competitor, and she gets the job done in spite of the extra load.

In the anchor position is a 10-year-old, who quickly takes the baton he has been anticipating the whole time and flies like the wind across the finish line to stop the clock.

We check the time: a new record!

Five seconds faster than the first service!

And the crowd goes wild!!

What could that intergenerational relay race possibly teach us about following Jesus in community?

As we will see below, the brain power we use to evaluate our experiences with physical objects in the physical world (like passing a baton) is some of the same brain power we borrow, and repurpose, and then use to understand and evaluate things like human communication or relationships (faith formation across generations being just one example).

But before we get to that, let's explore the ground rules of a physical relay race that we tend to uncritically adopt when we "pass on the faith" to the next generation.[3]

---

[2] It occurs to me that separation anxiety in a toddler is a good example of how we *embody* the metaphor Relational Distance is Physical Distance. When mom got up and moved farther away in *physical* space, the little boy experienced that distance as a threat to their *relationship*, and responded accordingly. The toddler didn't think about it, or imagine it, or try to construe Physical Distance as Relational Distance; he just started crying when mom left. That's how these *metaphors we live by* work; you don't consciously choose to think that way, you just think, feel, act, and justify your actions in terms that fit the metaphor.

[3] See *Preaching Metaphor: How to Shape Sermons that Shape People* by Justin Rossow for a more thorough description and analysis of "evoking the source" story and "mapping to the target" story in a sermon that used the Relay Race and Rope Team experiments in worship.

Ground Rules for a Relay Race

Let's notice some of the dynamics that seem so natural and obvious about that relay race. First, the individuals from different life stages certainly functioned *as a team*. Winning or losing was a group effort, and they were cheering for each other even when it wasn't their turn to run. The assumption that **(1) we are all in this together** positively carries over to the life of faith.

Second, each member of the group also had **(2) a direct, personal interaction** with the baton. That translates into our faith life as an individual, personal connection to faith in Jesus. Maybe you have heard it said, "God doesn't have grandkids." That's another way of describing how each member of the team in their different life stages still has a direct and personal connection to the baton. When we carry over that dynamic from the relay race to faith formation, we naturally assume each individual has a personal relationship with Jesus. While that relationship may be passed to them *from someone else*, it is still intimately *their own*. That's another helpful way of reasoning about faith formation.

But that's about where the helpful reasoning stops.

A third, uncritical assumption we can easily carry over has to do with the fundamentally *sequential* nature of the relay race. Although all of the individual runners are on the same team, for almost all of the race **(3) only one runner is running at a time**. In fact, the goal of the relay team is to make the amount of time two runners are running together as short has possible! The race will likely be won or lost based on how *quickly* and *efficiently* you get rid of the baton.

For a relay race, it makes good sense that the first runner runs the first leg of the race alone, and then hands off the baton as quickly as possible. Once that first leg has been run, the first runner can only cheer; no one would expect them to keep running. Now it's the second athlete's turn to run as best they can and pass of the baton as quickly as possible.

For a relay race, that logic makes sense. But when you carry those natural assumptions over to multigenerational discipleship, you get one generation who works as hard as they can to build the ministry of a local congregation, then hands off leadership and responsibility to the next generation as quickly

as possible. Once they are done with their part, they can cheer the next generation on, but **no one expects them to keep running.**

The generations three or four legs down the line have to wait their turn to handle the baton and make their contribution to the team. Start running too early, and the team will let you know you are obviously doing it wrong.

A relay race **only works in one set direction, in a predetermined path**: from Runner 1, to Runner 2, to Runner 3, etc. And if you step out of your lane, you are disqualified. That's the fourth uncritical assumption we often carry over to faith formation: it seems obvious and natural that passing the baton of faith should **(4a) only work in one direction,** from the wiser, older Christians to the younger or less experienced Christians. And **(4b) no deviation from previously set boundaries should be allowed, or you risk disqualification** (even if the out of bounds line is only imaginary).

Those four basic observations don't exhaust the list of relay race ground rules, but they do work together to make the standard procedure and clear goal of the whole relay team obvious: **we maximize individual effort while keeping the moment of passing the baton as brief as humanly possible, making sure no one crosses the boundary lines or drops the baton.**

While all the runners are on the same team, the actual running of the race involves independent, personal effort. The net result is merely a sum of the individual parts, where *helping others* during their part of the race is actually *against the rules*. And that fundamental thinking, feeling, and imagining shapes how we tend to uncritically view passing on the faith.

When multigenerational faith formation *doesn't* conform to the rules of the relay race, people tend to get frustrated, because their unspoken expectations aren't being met. The obvious and natural assumptions in our culture about "passing on the faith" make it seem natural and obvious for an older generation to be upset that younger generations don't want to take up the mantle and continue all the work they have done: Why won't they take the baton and run with it, the way they are supposed to? Why would they deviate from the norms we have already set? They are in danger of drifting out of our lane and disqualifying the whole team!

Younger generations can be confused and frustrated when leadership doesn't hand off important decisions or roles in the congregation: Why do they keep running with it when it is our turn? Why is passing the baton so inefficient? They need to let go, or we will never be able to move forward or run our leg of the race!

No one expects the youngest generations to contribute much, if anything, to the whole community; and no one expects the most experienced generations to need any help at all. In fact, offering help might even be illegal...

When it's their turn to run, each of the runners sprints as hard as they can, *all on their own*. They know they are on a team; they know they have a personal and individual relationship to Jesus; they know they have to keep the action of passing the baton as brief as possible; and they know they had better stay in their lane and not drop the baton!

Phew! That sounds exhausting!

As long as the way we bring people into a more mature faith conforms to the situation of "passing on the faith" like a physical baton in a physical relay race, our thoughts, emotions, imaginations, and logic will continue to reinforce both helpful and damaging assumptions about what we are trying to do as a multi-generational community of faith.

We aren't *trying* to see our life together this way; we just *do*.

Ask any member of the Body of Christ in North America if they think "intergenerational faith formation" is like a relay race, and they will probably look at you like a cow at a new gate. Or like a fish contemplating water.

But check their natural assumptions, uncritical reactions, default activity, and go-to logic and you will likely find people who *just know* that you pass faith *from* one generation *to* the next; that we're all on the same team, but running alone; that we all have a personal connection to faith in Jesus; and that more experienced generations don't need (or at least, *shouldn't* need) any support, while less experienced generations have little value to add (yet).

You will likely find people who feel a sense of failure that they didn't pass the baton better, a sense of anger that younger people have dropped the ball (or baton), and a fear that their local congregation and maybe even the whole

Church is at a crisis point because the whole team is in legitimate danger of losing, or even being disqualified. And there is plenty of blame to go around.

You will also likely find people who experience the pressure and burden and isolation of being expected to receive the faith from people who have already been running in a well-defined track, and to carry that faith successfully without stepping out of bounds, and to deliver that faith safely to the next generation without dropping the baton.

And to do all of that without help.

With their hands full.

While carrying a toddler suffering from separation anxiety.

I grieve for all the people in our churches who feel burdened and fearful, isolated and inadequate because the way we naturally frame passing down the faith makes those experiences seem obvious and natural. There's got to be something more to multigenerational faith formation than that.

A Little More about How We Think

I know; I know. If you are starting to feel a rising panic because the Church is failing to pass on the faith to the next generation, then a thought experiment about a relay race might seem trite and, honestly, pretty useless. We have a crisis on our hands! Who cares about track lanes and batons? Who cares how we *imagine* sharing the faith? Let's just *get it done*!

I hear you. And if you have gotten this far in a book about rethinking how we think, I hope you will suspect that **how we process a problem in the first place will in some ways predetermine what counts as a solution.**

If we actually want more people to trust Jesus for their eternal salvation and lean into dependence on Jesus in their day to day lives, then we have to get at the assumptions behind "passing on the faith" that are so obvious they go without saying. Because **what goes without saying can set the agenda in subtle ways we don't even notice.**

So let's take a moment to notice and explore together some of the dynamics that go into the ways we typically, naturally, and uncritically experience faith being passed from one person or generation to the next. We can shoot for a

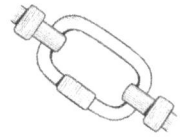

brief overview rather than an in-depth analysis, but we need some idea of how we are thinking, even if we don't usually stop to think about it.

If I can't look inside your heart, and you can't look inside mine, how do we evaluate or think about or draw conclusions about this subjective experience we call *faith*?[4] How do we *ever* come to grips with *any* abstractions, like thoughts, feelings, ideas, opinions, knowledge, or faith?

Let's see: you can *have* a thought, or *share* an emotion, or *pass on* some good advice. You can *hold onto* your opinion, *trade* insults, or *lose* your train of thought. You can *lock up* your feelings, *build on* your ideas, *preserve* your memories, or *pass on* your faith.

What's going on here?

It turns out, your brain has a nifty trick for processing all kinds of intangibles like thoughts, emotions, opinions, idea, and beliefs. **Your brain takes a reliable pattern of expectations and outcomes, learned from your experience with physical objects in the tangible world, and uses the same pattern to set default expectations and evaluate outcomes in situations you can't see or touch.**[5]

What you intuitively know about two kids playing catch with a ball (for example) gets translated into what seems obvious about two people tossing ideas back and forth (for example). The "*for examples*" are almost endless, because our experience with the physical world is ongoing, constantly reinforcing what we know about how physical objects behave in physical space. And we borrow that

---

[4] "The faith" can refer to the content of what you believe, often captured in creedal formulas. Right now we are talking about "faith," the personal experience of interacting with that content and holding it to be true.

[5] This trick of borrowing logic from one area of experience and repurposing it to process a different kind of experience is so much more than just *a way of talking* about one thing as if it were something else. Although there's still a lot we don't know about how the brain works, scientists have been able to demonstrate that our brains actually "borrow" neural networks used to process things like physical distance and *fire those same neurons* to process abstractions like relational or emotional "distance." See Carolyn Parkinson, Shari Liu, and Thalia Wheatley, "A Common Cortical Metric for Spatial, Temporal, and Social Distance," *The Journal of Neuroscience*, January 29, 2014, 34 (5):1979 –1987 for a concrete and specific example. See George Lakoff, "The Neural Theory of Metaphor" in Raymond Gibbs, ed., *The Cambridge Handbook of Metaphor and Thought* or Jerome Feldman, *From Molecule to Metaphor: A Neural Theory of Language* for a broader discussion of the general theory.

intuitive knowledge and apply it to a wide variety of abstract or subjective experiences all the time.

The concept of "passing on the faith" as if you were handling a physical object probably seems natural and obvious to most of us. It fits with other common phrases in our culture with similar logic, like "passing the mantle" or "passing the torch."

The pattern of thinking embedded in the physical action of *handling an object and giving it to someone else* makes some actions, attitudes, and decisions about faith formation seem natural and obvious. Some of those natural and obvious actions, attitudes, and decisions appropriate to "passing the mantle," or "passing the torch," or "passing on the faith" can be helpful: you want to feel like you are on the same team and that each individual has a personal relationship with Jesus.

But some of our natural assumptions about faith as passing on a baton can get important aspects of multigenerational faith formation terribly, terribly wrong. Isolation, inflexibility, and pressure to perform under threat of disqualification are not healthy parts of our life together as Church.

The answer isn't as easy as cutting a single phrase like "passing on the faith" from our vocabulary. **We will need some other ways of framing faith formation in community** that can expand our experience and give us other options for imagining faith and following.

Thankfully, the Scriptures give us a wide range of options when it comes to imagining and living out faith formation. For now, I want to look at one option in particular: the experience of *mountaineering on a rope team.*

Life on a Rope Team

If failing to "pass on" the faith, as if it were a physical object, amounts to "dropping the baton" on the Relay Race of Life, then our thoughts and emotions will guide how we reason about that tragic event. **As long as that Relay Race thinking is the only way we process the challenges of "passing on the faith," we will only find default answers that involve running harder or passing the baton**

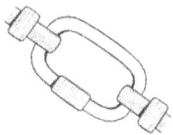

more effectively (while making sure everyone stays in bounds). So our goal is to find different ways to reframe faith formation, ways that preserve some of the most faithful aspects of our Relay Race default without making *isolating individual performance* seem like the only way forward.

Can we imagine something *more*, something that preserves the positive inferences of the Relay Race but also has the potential to expand what we know intuitively from the relay race, and reframe it into something more powerful, more beautiful, and more biblical in ways robust enough to displace the Relay Race as our primary lens for faith formation?[6] Let's give it a shot.

Take the five volunteers you recruited for the Relay Race experiment (whether real or imagined) and ask them to embody a different kind of logic. Instead of spacing them out and asking them to pass a baton, give them each a carabiner and have them all clip onto the same climbing rope.

You know what a carabiner is, right? You might have your keys or your lanyard on a big hook with a clip; that's a kind of carabiner. Carabiners are especially useful for securing a safety rope in rock climbing or mountaineering.

If you are hiking in a particularly dangerous area, or trekking across a glacier where snow and ice may be hiding a dangerous crevasse, you would likely want to be on a rope team. In mountaineering, a "rope team" is the small group of people who are all tied together to the same safety line.

---

[6] Relay Race assumptions tend to resist change in part because the Relay Race image not only draws on basic spatialization metaphors, it also coheres with one of the most fundamental and prevalent metaphors we live by in our culture: Life is a Journey.

Experiencing life as a kind of journey, you naturally become a traveler, and your goals seem to be destinations. Difficulties in life become obstacles you need to overcome with the help of guides, or vehicles, or fellow travelers. Major life decisions are framed as choosing between which path to take, and progress in life is measured in metaphorical distance and direction.

That way of framing the Journey of Life from birth to death is so entrenched in our language and our thinking, we rarely notice it. We don't just *talk* like that; we *live our lives* like that. And the Relay Race metaphor aligns easily with that primary way we imagine and experience Life. So Relay Race thinking will be persistent and well-hidden and seem to be *just the way it is*. Any metaphor that wants to compete for primacy in our conceptual system will need to match the Relay Race's connection to powerful assumptions in our culture.

To geek out on Life is a Journey, see "The contemporary theory of metaphor" by George Lakoff in A. Ortony, ed., *Metaphor and Thought;* George Lakoff and Mark Turner, *More than Cool Reason: A Field Guide to Poetic Metaphor*; Zoltán Kövecses, *Metaphor: A Practical Introduction;* and Mark Turner, *The Literary Mind: The Origins of Thought and Language*.

The idea is simple: if one person takes a dangerous fall, the people ahead of them *and behind them* on the rope are committed to their safety and recovery. (In your experiment, ask someone in the middle of the rope line to fall down in slow motion; notice the effect that fall has on the whole team.)

If you stumble or fall, it doesn't matter whether you are in second position or fourth, the people *on either side of you* are committed to you. In the same way, you are committed to both of them. The group supports each individual, and each individual supports the group.

As your volunteers pantomime some mountaineering across imaginary obstacles in the front of your sanctuary, see what kinds of decisions and emotions become natural and obvious to them as a group.

Are the mountaineers still **(1) all in this together,** like the relay team was? Certainly! That positive inference from the Relay Race frame is carried over by the Rope Team. In fact, being on the same rope may highlight the companionship of our faith walk even more than the team aspect of the relay race: not only does the whole team compete together and win or lose as a team, **they actually travel together and participate together and depend on each other throughout the expedition.**

Does each member of our faith rope team still experience **(2) a direct, personal interaction** with faith and following? Would it still be true to say that God doesn't have grandkids? Well, each individual has a personal connection to the rope, while the rope joins them all together. The carabiner serves as a reminder that there is an **individual aspect** to the journey of faith, while the unique carabiners simultaneously serve an **overarching unity.**

Does mountaineering assume each individual is **(3) acting in isolation** except for brief, critical moments of interacting with others? No! Decidedly not! The standard operating procedure on a rope team is to do all of the *dangerous* stuff *together*. You might find moments of individual activity "off the rope," but those moments would only be in the least critical or dangerous situations. Mountaineering with a rope team, by definition, means **you all move forward together.**

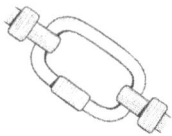

Does traversing a glacier or climbing a cliff entail **(4a) one set direction and path?** No again! Although you are certainly heading in a specific direction on a mountaineering expedition, you don't necessarily have **(4b) a single, defined path you must take, or risk being disqualified.** As the trek presents unique challenges or opportunities, the group might take an alternate route, or have to backtrack to get around an obstacle, or go out of their way for a particularly beautiful view. While traveling on a rope team means you are all traveling together, **it doesn't insist on predetermined route.**[7]

Depending on what happens along the way, any one of the members of the rope team may end up leading or following any other member; and in times of uncertainty, you look both ahead and behind for support.

That logic of mountaineering on a rope team opens up new possibilities for your life of faith. The more experienced generation is not "done" once they have "passed the baton." Less experienced followers do not need to become experts before they can take their turn to run with the faith. **Everyone has something to learn, and something to share.** The order of the adventure hikers doesn't determine who needs help or who gets help: you are committed to people both ahead of you and behind you. And if you stumble or fall, you can **look for and expect help from both directions.**

Faith, in Both Directions

That kind of relational thinking has taken a burden off of my own parenting. It has opened me up to the possibility of receiving support *from* my children

---

[7] Notice how the Rope Team image aligns with Life is a Journey just as well as the Relay Race does. In fact, at some key points, the Rope Team opens up options within the Life is a Journey metaphor that the Relay Race shuts down. In some kinds of journeys, there is only *one path* and you can only move *forward*, or your journey is a failure; the Relay Race is a Journey like that. But the Rope Team Journey allows for the fact that detours, backtracking, scenic routes, and going off the beaten path are also options for how we reason about and process living Life. That's why I think the Rope Team has a chance of supplanting the Relay Race in our hearts and minds and imaginations: the Rope Team also aligns with Life is a Journey, but in ways that relieve the Relay Race burden of having to stay in bounds, always get it right, only move in one direction, and only depend on yourself.

instead of expecting faith to move in only one direction, from me (the more experienced believer) to my kids (the less experienced).

When one of my teenage daughters asks a question about Scripture or about what we believe, I used to feel like I had better get "the right answer" so I didn't drop the baton. But if my teenage daughters are "on my rope" then we are in this together, and we can discover more about Scripture or about what we believe, together; and I am allowed to learn something, too.

When I mess up in my parenting, I am no longer afraid to admit my shortcoming to my kids. I don't have pressure to perform up to Olympic standards; I just get to stumble along, with people on my rope to help. I am able to see help coming from people who know more and have experienced more than I have; and I can also see real help coming from my kids themselves.

I'm not just in charge of strengthening *their* faith; my kids are also committed to helping strengthen *mine*.

I learn more about what Jesus is up to in my life as I listen to their insights and hear their prayers and talk with them about their struggles as well as my own. **This intergenerational interaction is less about delivering the faith to my kids, and more about discovering more about Jesus, together.**

Viewing the next generation *already now* as participants on this journey of faith can take some of the pressure off of a single faith conversation or moment of passing the baton. (Have you ever dreaded having *The Talk* with your kids about believing in Jesus, or going to church, or reading the Bible? Like, if we get this one interaction wrong, we could mess up our kids for life! Yikes!)

As parents and grandparents and neighbors and friends, we're in this for the long haul, and even if there are some challenges or detours, we are committed to walking together.

That means, there is no single conversation you have to get right to help young people in your congregation or family know and follow Jesus; you just keep having faith conversations. Make time and proximity a priority,

The blessings of "being on the same rope" instead of "passing down the faith" became clear to me when our youngest (the boy) was still quite young. As I was trying to instill in him the value of trusting God's promises, I ran an

experiment for a few weeks: every night before bed, I made the sign of the cross on his forehead and on his heart with the baptismal words: "Receive the sign of the cross on your forehead and on your heart to mark you as one redeemed by Christ, the Crucified."

I know: probably a bit wordy for a little kid, but I was just experimenting. And the physical touch and unusual words had their intended effect. My son started expecting that blessing at night before bed.

And then it happened.

Having seen the importance I placed on that action of blessing, my little boy wanted to return the gesture. He didn't get all the words right, but he drew me close and made the sign of the cross on *my* forehead and on *my* heart to remind *me* that I was also one redeemed by Christ, the Crucified.

If Relay Race was the only mode of faith formation available to me, I would have thought that tender gesture was perhaps sweet; but I would have naturally and automatically discounted those words on the lips of my young son because *you only pass the baton of faith in one direction.*

I am thankful that I had already been shaped to think in terms of needing people ahead of me *and behind me* on the journey of faith. Because I saw my little boy as someone "on my rope," even though he was maybe six at the time, I could receive his faltering words and clear gestures as a real promise for my tired and struggling faith.

He didn't need to understand all the grownup stress, or adult heartache, or habitual sins, or ongoing disappointments of trying to be a good pastor, and husband, and dad; he just took the promise he received and gave it back to me.

And I have to tell you, *it counted*. Those words weren't just *cute*. They called out a response of faith in me. They made me want to believe. They invited and empowered my own trust, and repentance, and joyful faith.

I spoke a promise to a child and didn't even know my faith was stumbling until that young and inexperienced disciple helped me get back on my feet and take a next step. That's what intergenerational discipleship is all about: seeking to speak promises to the next generation in ways that invite them to speak promises right back. We are in this together. We need each other.

In his farewell sermon, Moses warned God's people not to let forgetfulness sever the bond of faith from one generation to the next. But the words Moses uses sound more like mountaineering than running a relay race: "Talk about these covenant promises when you sit in your house, and **when you walk by the way**, and when you lie down, and when you rise" (Deuteronomy 6:7).

The task of perpetuating faith to the next generation does not get lived out in a few critical moments of passing the baton; multigenerational faith formation takes place day after day, in big ways and small, over the course of years and decades. And we desperately need the support of the next generation as much they need us.

. . .

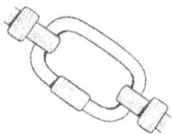

Summary of Chapter 4: Relay Race or Rope Team?

The way we typically think about "passing on the faith" highlights the common interest of the community and the personal nature of each individual's faith. That's good. But that Relay Race mentality also isolates generations from each other and allows for faith to move in only one direction, from the older generation to the younger.

More helpful, faithful, and beautiful ways of imagining multi-generational faith formation include framing life as a communal journey where we walk together on a Rope Team. On the rope, we expect to give and receive help in either direction. Mutual support over time becomes an obvious and natural part of multi-generational faith formation.

This Changes Everything

Relay Race   Rope Team

	Relay Race	Rope Team
Jesus	Your personal relationship with Jesus is the baton you pass on to the next generation, so that they also have a personal relationship with him; they have to "make the faith their own."	You have a personal relationship with Jesus because you are connected to the rope; being connected to Jesus, by definition, means you are connected to other people connected to Jesus.
The Church	A combination of track coach (teaches you how to run the race) and line judge (tells you when you are out of bounds).	A "walking with" community that looks for where Jesus is, and where Jesus is headed. People on the move.
The World	Obstacles, impediments, or even enemies (fight the good fight = finish the race).	A place to be explored, but with the safety of other people on your rope. Dangerous, but beautiful and full of adventure.
The Goal	Complete the race as quickly as possible; pass the baton as quickly as possible.	Stay connected to other people. Explore great beauty. Take a next step with other people.
My Role	Stay in bounds. Run my leg as fast as I can. Leave the person behind me quickly. Pass off my responsibility and my faith to the next generation, so they can run with it, leaving me behind.	Give support to people ahead of me *and* behind me on the journey. Receive support from people both ahead of me *and* behind me. Stay connected. Keep walking together.
Key Thinking	I look in one direction and go as fast as I can. Although we are all on the same team, our time together is designed to be as short as possible. Stay in bounds.	Who's on my rope? Who is supporting me? Who can I support? We don't move forward unless we move forward together.

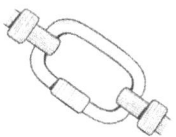

For Further Reflection

Run a relay race with your group. Then tie onto the same rope and climb over some obstacles. Compare and contrast those two different experiences.

Who's on your rope? How do you know?

What do you do if it feels like you don't have anyone on your rope?

What elements of your congregation or family life seem to follow most closely the patterns and expectations of a Relay Race mentality?

What would have to change in your life if you were to experience multigenerational faith formation as a Rope Team?

What other biblical images for intergeneration faith do you find engaging?

Chapter 5

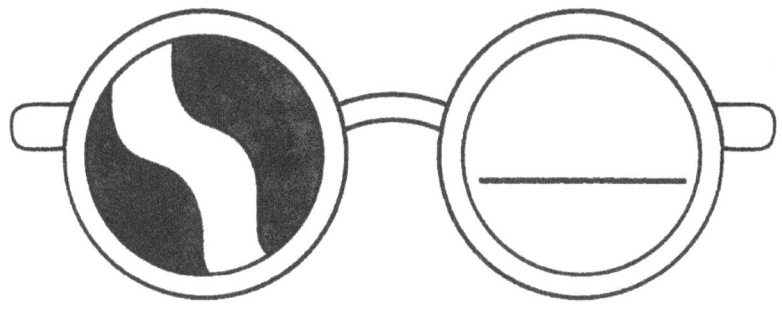

What You See is What You Get
The Wisdom of Changing Your Lenses

Looking Back to Move Forward

As we saw in the last chapter, when we operate solely within the parameters of a Relay Race, certain emotions, expectations, and evaluations about discipleship seem completely natural and obvious to us. But those "natural" and "obvious" implications for passing on the faith *change dramatically* if we shift to a Rope Team mindset. What's up with that?

The *metaphors we live by* (like the Relay Race or Rope Team) often go unnoticed because they seem so obvious and natural. At the same time, these metaphorical lenses affect what we see and therefore how we think we should respond. They filter our experience, our logic, our expectations, our actions, and the way we evaluate our actions.

Before we move on, let's take a moment to look closer at how and why that filtering takes place. Once we start to notice our own default settings for discipleship, we can begin to reframe our natural assumptions and obvious reactions in more biblical (and more beautiful) ways. A quick look back will help us move forward.

We started to see metaphor's impact on discipleship way back in the opening chapter: the difference between an Assembly Line mindset and Adventure thinking comes down to which metaphor is filtering the expectations, obvious

actions, and ground rules for engagement. Do you think you are you *making* standardized disciples in an efficient, professional environment? Or are you *walking with* people as they grow along the way? **Different metaphors naturally lead to different actions.**

Chapter 2 (Fish Discover Water Last) expanded on that initial insight. Do you remember the Wild Beast and Virus experiment? How subjects *discounted the metaphor* at the same time it was shaping their thinking about crime and how to stop it? **Even when it doesn't feel like it, the metaphor you use to interpret any given situation makes a huge difference in what you think is going on** (and how you feel about it, and what you think you should do about it). That, in a nutshell, is what's going on with all of the discipleship metaphors we've looked at so far.

The difference in Chapter 3 between setting a High Bar (as if you were an athlete trying to reach Up to a standard) and looking for the Spirit to come Down and form your faith (as if you were a Clay Jar) flows directly from the different orientation and expectations inherent in those two very different metaphors, and in the very different situations they evoke. Your job is either to strive upward or to look for the Spirit to come down and shape you. What you think you are doing will affect what you actually do.

Similarly, the contrast (in the last chapter) between experiencing faith formation as a kind of *relay race* and imagining the people around you as fellow travelers *on your rope* is exactly the contrast between the two dissimilar situations those disparate metaphors invite us to live out. We'll see this same dynamic in the rest of the book, as well: **the way you live out your faith is shaped in profound ways by the metaphors you choose to live by.**

It's almost hard to believe *metaphors* are so important for ongoing discipleship because, if we notice them at all, we tend to disregard metaphors as "figures of speech," ornamental or poetic language meant to embellish (or even deceive). But the metaphors that reside (and often hide) in our conceptual system will filter how we experience, imagine, and live out our ordinary lives of faith, both as individuals and in community. The present chapter takes a closer look at how that filtering actually works.

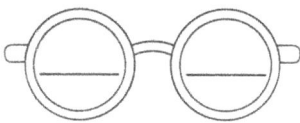

The Situational Logic of Relays and Rope Teams

The secret to metaphor's hidden power to set expectations, evaluations, emotions, and actions boils down to one thing: **borrowed situational logic.** We take what we know *about one situation*—all the appropriate inferences, feelings, potential outcomes, obstacles, helpers, goals, etc.—and borrow those complex relationships and extrapolations to understand, experience, and act in *a different situation*.[1] The differences between the implicit situations of a Relay Race and Rope Team from the previous chapter make a good example.

Think about it for a minute: if you were running a relay race, and you took a nasty spill, what would your natural reaction be *in that situation?* What would your thoughts and emotions tell you about what you are supposed to do next? I imagine I would get back up as quickly as I could, in spite of the pain, and run as fast as I could, to try and make up for lost time. You, too?

If you fell in the middle of a competition, would you maybe feel like you let other people down? Or that you are a failure? Those feelings might seem natural and obvious. Would you be angry with yourself or ashamed of your lack of skill? That would make sense.

In that kind of competitive setting, sitting on the track with a bruised ankle and a skinned knee, would it even occur to you to look for help?

---

[1] The history of metaphor interpretation is an exploration of how different thinkers have tried to describe this process of understanding one thing (or situation) in terms of something else. Theories based on similarity or comparison can't quite account for what's actually going on in metaphor. Max Black's Interaction Theory has a lot to commend it, though his language of Tenor and Vehicle is no longer widely used. The metaphor theory characterized by Lakoff and Johnson talks about "mapping" from the Source Domain to the Target Domain.

Mark Turner, in *The Literary Mind*, captures the narrative or situational dynamic of metaphor. He talks about "story" and "projection" from one domain to another as the heart of metaphor. Richard M. White, coming from an entirely different direction, ends up with a similar conclusion when he talks about the "appropriate situation" behind a metaphor in *The Structure of Metaphor: The Way the Language of Metaphor Works*.

My own attempt to describe the story, situation, or narrative structure inherent in metaphor gets its most thorough and theoretical treatment in "Preaching the Story Behind the Image: A Narrative Approach to Metaphor for Preaching" Ph. D. diss., Concordia Seminary—St. Louis, 2009. If you want to get a handle on how a variety of theories of metaphor interpretation all relate to each other, check out the Appendix; it's a hoot.

Well, *no:* because you know that it would violate the rules of the race for others to cross into your lane and give you a hand.

You have limited options as long as you are in the Relay Race situation: you can either give up on the race entirely and receive medical attention, or else you are on your own to do the best you can to make up for your mistake, though doing well in the race is no longer an option. You can reasonably expect your teammates to be disappointed, and maybe even angry at your performance; and you are, too.

What you think is supposed to happen next, what options you see in front of you, what you expect from other people and from yourself, what your emotions are telling you about yourself, how you evaluate what just happened and how you imagine the near future—all of that is tied up in your understanding of how relay races and competitions work. In a very real sense, what you see is what you get.

If the Relay Race situation is the story or situation you use to structure your experience of faith and following, what happens when you take a nasty spill? When your children see you fail to perform up to the standard your parents set for you? When your sins of omission are painfully obvious, both to your mentors and to the new or young believers in your life? When temptation trips you up and you find yourself flat on your face?

As long as you are "passing on the faith to the next generation," your thoughts, emotions, and expectations will conform to the rules of engagement that flow so naturally from a Relay Race. That situational logic automatically kicks in. Without taking time to consider why, you will feel ashamed of your failure and instinctively know you have two choices: get up on your own and work hard to make up for lost time, or give up on the race.

Of course you don't expect *help* from the people on your relay team; you expect disappointment, and blame, and maybe even anger. You think, feel, and act according to the rules of the Relay Race experience.

But what if you are living out your faith walk as if it were a mountaineering adventure instead of passing the baton? What if you are part of a Rope Team instead of a Relay Race? Then, when you inevitably take a nasty spill, your

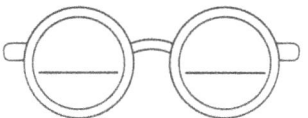

thoughts, emotions, and actions look and feel different because **the situation, and therefore the logic of the situation, has shifted.**

On a Rope Team, your fall may even be your fault, but the focus isn't really on placing blame at all. When someone on your rope team slips, the people on either side immediately know about it; and they immediately take action.

You wouldn't expect disappointment or shame or anger from your traveling companions; you do expect help! *Trying to get up all on your own* isn't even a viable option, although you do cling tightly to the rope that binds you all together. The fall may still be painful, but the pain as well as the danger is naturally and automatically dealt with *in community* rather than in isolation.

What if following Jesus were like that?

What if the more mature believer you look up to and the child or friend you want to encourage in the faith were both walking with you on this journey of faith in a way that makes it natural and obvious *for both of them to come to your aid* if you stumble or fall?

What if it seemed natural and obvious for you to be there *for either of them* in their moment of need?

What if your sin or struggle didn't push people away and leave you isolated, but drew your team around you as they automatically seek to help you back to your feet?

What if you could receive a blessing from your child as if from the mouth of God? What if your Bible study leader was also permitted to desperately need *your* prayers, even though they are more experienced in the faith than you are?

What would change in your life if you experienced multi-generational faith formation as a mountaineering Rope Team instead of an Olympic Relay Race?

Because the logic of those two very different *situations* leads to a whole range of different assumptions, emotions, and actions, your experience of relational discipleship would be characterized by a very different set of obvious answers, natural outcomes, and unquestionable goals.

What you see is what you get.

Building a More Biblical Collage

I think the Rope Team paradigm for discipling is way more engaging, way more beautiful, and much more fun than running a Relay Race and facing the challenge of passing the baton. When you get right down to it, I think the Rope Team is probably even more *biblical* than the Relay Race; not that Paul or Jesus would have known what a carabiner is, but because the situational logic of the Rope Team seems to conform in significant ways to the situational logic of metaphors the Scriptures use to talk about discipleship in community.[2]

The biblical language of "discipling" (as a verb, not as an end product) is more an image of *walking with, over time,* than a standard process that always produces a standard result. That biblical concept of walking with over time aligns with the situational logic of a Rope Team. In contrast, a Relay Race values some of the same elements highlighted by the Assembly Line: standardization, professionalization, efficiency, and speed. Isolation is just a natural part of the process.

But even if we can agree that the Rope Team aligns with more biblical ways of thinking and living than the Relay Race mentality does, that doesn't make walking together on a rope team "right" and passing down the faith like a baton "wrong." Different metaphors for faith and following are like **snapshots of a beautiful landscape taken from different perspectives.** Each snapshot can provide unique and therefore valuable information from one particular perspective. But to comprehend the whole, we need more than even our favorite snapshot. **We need a collage of metaphors to help express the fullness of our life together in Christ.**

Maybe, for some situations, passing the baton is a helpful model. I mean, doesn't the phrase "passing the mantle" actually come from the Bible?? (See Elijah and Elisha in 2 Kings 2.) And of course, Hebrews 12 can tell us to "run the race" set before us, just as Paul can tell his young friend Timothy, "I have finished the race" (2 Timothy 4:7).

---

[2] I believe situational logic is the key to "translating" a metaphor from one language or culture to another. See my discussion of an example sermon on "Thy Word is a lamp to my feet" in *The Pastor's Brain Manual: A Fascinating Work in Progress,* ed. Allen Nauss, 104-131.

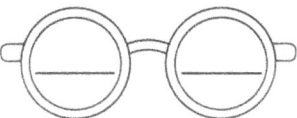

So it's not that all talk about Faith as an Object or Life as a Race is *wrong* or *unbiblical*. But as a default, go-to, standard way of living out our faith, the Relay Race metaphor, even when we don't notice it, leads us to think, feel, imagine, and take action in ways that can leave us isolated and exhausted.

The Rope Team image, on the other hand, seems to capture a reciprocal relationship I think the Bible is after (as in Romans 1: "That you and I may be mutually encouraged by each other's faith"). **You might need the perspective of either snapshot at any given point on your journey of faith; but you also need the collage that holds both of them together.**

You could even suggest that the Rope Team is more central or important to the collage than the Relay Race is. But that doesn't make it necessarily "better;" just more helpful in more situations.

We have other biblical options for reframing relational discipleship. As but one example, a host of horticultural images dealing with planting, watering, bearing fruit, etc. could provide fertile ground for thinking differently.

Paul says, "I planted the seed, Apollos watered it, but God has been making it grow" (1 Corinthians 3:6, NIV).

Jesus says, "This is what the kingdom of God is like. A man scatters seed on the ground. Night and day, whether he sleeps or gets up, the seed sprouts and grows, though he does not know how" (Mark 4:25-27, NIV).

And, of course, Jesus tells the disciples in the Upper Room: "I am the vine; you are the branches. If you remain in me and I in you, you will bear much fruit; apart from me you can do nothing" (John 15:5, NIV).

What if we were to add that "planting and watering and mysteriously growing over time" snapshot to our collage? What if we also *cultivated faith* in our homes and congregations instead of just *passing it on*?

As long as we only have one, default snapshot for any area of Christian faith or life, we will only find answers and make decisions that seem obvious from that one, specific, default perspective, at the expense of the collage.

Noticing, exploring, adding to, and sometimes even changing out the metaphors we most often live by will open up new possibilities and give us some new "obvious" responses to the ongoing challenges of faith and following.

The Invitation to Change Your Lens

Viewing your faith through the lens of a different metaphor will allow you to see things differently. And what you see will affect what you think is going on, what you expect to happen next, and what you think you should do about it.

Changing metaphors is kind of like taking off your sunglasses and putting on a pair of reading glasses: you wear those different lenses at different times for different reasons. **Swapping your sunglasses for reading glasses entails both seeing things differently and changing what you think you are doing.**

In a sense, that's what we are being asked to do with the way we typically see (and therefore live out) *discipleship*. We are being invited to trade in one set of standard lenses for a different way of filtering the faith. But this invitation to change your perspective is nothing new; it's actually very biblical.

One of my favorite instances of Jesus asking his disciples to change the metaphors they live by comes in the story of the Samaritan woman at the well. Or, more properly, it comes in the story embedded in parenthesis wrapped within the story of the woman at the well.

In the First Century, the region of Judea (the area surrounding Jerusalem and Bethlehem) was separated from the northern region of Galilee (and towns like Nazareth and Capernaum) by the foreign territory of Samaria. For lots of historical, political, and religious reasons, there was no love lost between the Jews and Samaritans, even though (and perhaps, especially because) they shared some of the same blood.

In John 4, Jesus is heading from the region of Judea in the south back to his home region of Galilee in the north. But unlike most Jewish travelers of the day, Jesus doesn't skirt Samaria to the east; he leads his disciples right into this enemy-occupied territory. That's where we find Jesus unexpectedly talking to a Samaritan woman at lunch time. But as soon as we meet the Samaritan woman, John tells us (in parentheses) why Jesus is all alone at the well.

> A woman from Samaria came to draw water. Jesus said to her, "Give me a drink." (For his disciples had gone away into the city to buy food.)
>
> John 4:7-8 (ESV)

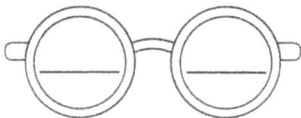

That little detail is more telling than it seems at first blush. This question of lunch comes up again when the disciples return and are surprised to find Jesus talking to this Samaritan woman (who herself was surprised that Jesus would talk to her in the first place).

> Meanwhile the disciples were urging him, saying, "Rabbi, eat."
> But he said to them, "I have food to eat that you do not know about."
> So the disciples said to one another, "Has anyone brought him something to eat?"

John 4:31-33 (ESV)

To my American ears, it kind of sounds like the disciples are concerned that they might have wasted their money on an extra Big Mac meal; if Jesus got lunch on his own, then we didn't need to bring him takeout!

But (surprise!), that's not what is going on here at all.

John has already told us (again, in parentheses) that Jews refuse to have anything to do with Samaritans; that's one reason the woman is startled when Jesus asks her for a drink. But that's just part of the story.

Jews and Samaritans *hated* each other. And good Jews wanted to make sure they were clearly distinct from their ethnically-related enemies. That's why most Jews would have gone out of their way to avoid Samaria altogether.

In the first century, one of the clearest ways of maintaining their difference from all other nations, and especially the Samaritans, had to do with food laws: what you could eat and how you could eat it.

We'll look more at community boundary markers in Chapter 6 and our assumptions about enemies in Chapter 7. For now, you need to know that *food* was a clear boundary marker in Jesus' day: his disciples were not only surprised to find him talking to a Samaritan woman, they were aghast at the thought that somebody else, specifically *someone from Samaria*, might have given Jesus something defiling to eat.

It must have been almost as if, having returned from the only kosher deli in the entire village, they found Jesus calmly polishing off a ham sandwich. It would have been shocking, confusing, and maybe even disgusting.

So here in John 4, behind Samaritan lines,[3] the disciples are viewing their situation through a pair of standard issue field glasses that make *identity* and *purity* the key elements. They naturally assume all Samaritans are enemies who pose a threat their Jewish purity and therefore to their Jewish identity. That's when Jesus invites his disciples to see through a new lens.

> The disciples said to one another, "Has anyone brought him something to eat?" Jesus said to them, "My food is to do the will of him who sent me and to accomplish his work. Do you not say, 'There are yet four months, then comes the harvest'? Look, I tell you, lift up your eyes, and see that the fields are white for harvest."
>
> John 4:33-35 (ESV)

I think it must have been important because Jesus says it three times in three different ways, for emphasis: Look! Lift up your eyes! See! Jesus is asking his disciples to take their default snapshot, with its emphasis on purity and enemies, and replace it with a different lens, a new way of looking at this situation—and therefore a new way of reasoning, feeling, and acting in this situation.

Jesus resets their expectations and concerns. Jesus adjusts their perspective. Jesus invites them to live in a reality defined in terms of *fields ripe for harvest* rather than *keeping separate from defiling enemies*.

And it seems to work! At least, a little. The disciples still have a lot of growing to do.[4] (Don't we all?) But already in John 4, these disciples find themselves with a different set of lenses, and therefore a different kind of response.

---

[3] I don't think it is stating it too strongly to say that the disciples saw this Samaritan village as nothing less than enemy-occupied territory. We catch a glimpse of the disciples' default position in the rather obscure little scene in Luke 9 when Jesus turns his face toward Jerusalem, and for that reason alone, he and his entourage are not welcome at the next Samaritan Motel 6. The Sons of Thunder (James and John) immediately jump to Shock and Awe: "Lord, do you want us to call down fire from heaven to consume them?!" If Samaria is enemy-occupied territory, then acts of war seem like a reasonable response to provocation.

[4] Later, in Acts 8, the Jerusalem church will hear about believers in Samaria. They send Peter and John to investigate (James has already been martyred). On this trip across the border, the disciples actually lay hands on the Samaritan believers and pray for the Holy Spirit. (Talk about calling down fire from heaven!)

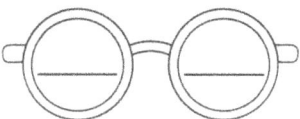

This time, when the woman comes back with the rest of the village, these kosher disciples with their complicated dietary restrictions are prepared to follow Jesus and spend two more days in that foreign town—something no good Jew at the time would likely have dreamt of doing.

Notice that Jesus invites these disciples to change their primary way of seeing and understanding and feeling and reasoning about Samaritans *right in the middle of a complex and emotional situation*: as they are facing a potentially threatening crowd of approaching Samaritans! I suspect that kind of shift in perspective often happens precisely in the moments when worldviews collide.

Because those kinds of moments are often filled with risk and uncertainty, reframing the way we experience faith and following can feel dangerous or threatening. But because Jesus is the one inviting us to reconsider our default ways of viewing the world, we can trust the Spirit is active in the process.

In the case of those disciples who encountered a crowd of unknown Samaritans on the wrong side of the border, a new way of seeing (and therefore living out) the situation in front of them led to something unexpected. Over the next couple of days, that whole village of "enemy outsiders" came to faith in Jesus as the Savior of the world (John 4:42).

Not every situation you find yourself in as a follower of Jesus will end up just like that. At times, you may experience "outsiders" as "enemies." As we will see in Chapter 7, the Bible has ways for talking about that experience; even *that* snapshot belongs in the collage. But in John 4, Jesus is saying, for *this particular situation*, "enemies" is the wrong view to take; the wrong snapshot to preference; the wrong lens through with to filter the situation in front of you. If you experience these Samaritans as "defiling outsiders," you will miss what's actually going on.

The challenge is not merely in collecting "correct" biblical snapshots to add to your collage; it's **discerning which lens is appropriate for which situation.**

When Jesus invites his disciples to "look, lift up your eyes, and see" he is asking them to trade out their default *purity* and *enemy* filters for a pair of lenses he calls "the fields are white for harvest." The emotions, inferences, expectations, actions, and assumptions that go with the "fields white for

harvest" glasses are very different from the emotions, inferences, expectations, actions, and assumptions that go with "defiling, enemy outsiders."

Jesus isn't saying the disciples will *never* experience enemies on their journey of faith; but if the disciples apply the situational logic of enemies by default to *this particular situation in front of them,* their thoughts, feelings, and actions will not align with the heart of God.

Wisdom and Assumptions

When we finally get around to talking about what goes without saying, when we begin to notice some of the default metaphors we automatically and uncritically live by, we've got a couple of choices. The first, and by far easier option, is to replace our old standard default with a new (and presumably better) one.

Is an industrial inclination toward standardization, professionalization, and efficiency hurting the Church? Then let's never use an Assembly Line mentality again and only adopt the values and inferences of an Adventure to think about our new member classes! Is the Relay Race of faith isolating generations? Get rid of it! From now on, only Rope Team thinking is allowed!

This kind of one-for-one exchange could in some situations actually be good for the faith walk of real individuals and communities. An Adventure mindset really *is* a better way to structure faith formation than an Assembly Line; we actually *do* follow Jesus better when we follow him together, and don't limit multigenerational faith formation to one bright shining moment of passing the baton.

But an even better answer than merely changing our old default for a new one is getting into the regular habit of checking our assumptions. The more snapshots we have in our collage, the more options we will see for thinking, feeling, imagining the future, and responding to the situation in front of us.

Walking With may be better for the individual and the community, and much closer to what Jesus had in mind, than Assembly Line thinking; but are you supposed to get rid of all talk of efficiency or standardization? If you use

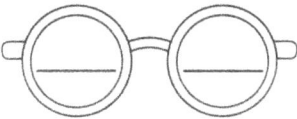

any creed or confession of faith, wouldn't you want at least *some* of your new member class to have a semblance of standardization?

Limiting discipleship to the "professionals" may have negative effects on the whole process. At the same time, wouldn't you want your professional church workers to have some kind of connection to the faith lives of people in your congregation? Wouldn't you want them to know your new members?

Christian mentoring is clearly one-sided; a more-experienced believer shares perspective and insight with a less-experienced believer. But the Rope Team mindset is much healthier for the Church than some kind of Relay Race.

Does that mean we get rid of all mentoring? Stop any age-related groups or activities? Ask the third grade Sunday School teacher to start bringing the kids to the Adult Bible Class?

The problem with simply replacing your old, default metaphor for a new way of viewing faith and following is this: ***any* metaphor will both highlight and hide important aspects of the situation in front of you.**[5] Even on a mountaineering expedition, a more experienced member might show a newbie the ropes; even an adventure will benefit from some kind of routine.

So the more difficult, but far better approach, is to develop the habit of noticing your default metaphors and adopt a practice of checking your filter to see what assumptions seem "obvious" or "natural" and why. Look at the challenge or question or relationship in front of you, and notice the snapshot you are automatically using; then, check the collage. You might find another snapshot that makes different actions seem reasonable, different outcomes appear possible, and different ways of thinking and feeling seem natural and appropriate in this particular situation.

During a recent eclipse, my son's school handed out special "eclipse glasses" you could use to look directly at the solar phenomenon. I joined him and his class (and the whole school) out on a sports field for the special event. The daylight turned shadowy and surreal as we all held flimsy cardboard frames with impossibly dark lenses pressed up against our faces.

---

[5] See especially Chapter 3, "Metaphorical Systematicity: Highlight and Hiding" in *Metaphors We Live By* (Lakoff and Johnson, 1980; 2003).

If I try to use those same eclipse glasses now to read my computer better as I type, I actually can't see anything at all; they are way too dark to be of any use. But if I had tried to use a pair of reading glasses to look directly at the solar eclipse, that wouldn't have worked well, either. (Ouch!)

But using the eclipse glasses to do what they were designed to do, to look at the sun, we were able to watch that heavenly event unfold. The trick isn't just to notice what metaphors you live by; it's to **decide which metaphor shapes a faithful way of living in** *this particular situation.*

In that sense, changing your lenses or checking your snapshot against your collage is a lot like living out what the book of Proverbs would call Wisdom.

Proverbs are often succinct sayings that contain wisdom for living, but proverbs also *require wisdom* to put into practice. "Look before you leap" is a proverbial saying (though not biblical). But so is, "He who hesitates is lost."

Biblical proverbs are wise and pithy sayings like that. And sometimes, even in the Bible, even in back-to-back verses, you can get what seems like contradictory advice:

> Don't answer the foolish arguments of fools,
>   or you will become as foolish as they are.
> Be sure to answer the foolish arguments of fools,
>   or they will become wise in their own estimation.
>
> Proverbs 26:4-5 (NIV)

So which is it? Am I supposed to answer a foolish argument? Or is it wise not to? Am I supposed to slow down long enough to make sure this important decision doesn't have unintended negative consequences? (Look before you leap.) Or am I in danger of missing this unique opportunity by slowing down too much? (He who hesitates is lost.)

Which is it? The answer, or course, is: *it depends on the situation.*

Each wisdom saying on its own contains an insight or guiding principle, but the real wisdom comes in knowing which wise saying is the right one for the context in front of you.

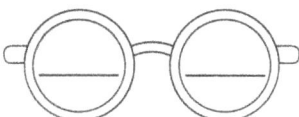

In some instances, it would be *wise* to live out the adage, "He who hesitates is lost." But if you apply that principle automatically and uncritically, you will run into some of the very good reasons why "Look before you leap" is also wise.

In some situations, it's better not to respond (Facebook tirade, maybe?). But sometimes you need to say something to keep the situation from getting worse. So how do you know which proverb applies to this specific situation?

There isn't an *easy* answer; there is only a *wise* one.

Deciding which snapshot from the broader biblical collage of images should shape your living in *this particular instance* works like that. There is no single, obvious, easy answer. (Though some answers are better than others.) You try on one set of colored glasses and view the world one way; then you try on a different set of lenses to see what becomes obvious and natural. You choose between Relay Race and Rope Team, between Assembly Line and Adventure, between High Bar and Clay Jar, and then you try living out your life in community with those filters in place.

But here's the catch: **when you are wearing colored glasses all the time, it's easy to forget you are wearing colored glasses at all.** When you only have one snapshot, the collage is reduced to a single perspective.

And as long as that single perspective is running the show, it won't *feel like* you need a different perspective. But you know better.

Wisdom recognizes the snapshot, and doesn't lose sight of the collage. Wisdom knows when to use reading glasses, and when eclipse glasses would help you see more clearly.

So when you go to restructure your new member process, it's good to think more in terms of Rope Team than Relay Race; it's good to think Clay Jar, not High Bar; it's good to think Adventure, not Assembly Line. The natural assumptions, goals, inferences, and emotions embedded in the Rope Team, Clay Jar, and Adventure images are more biblical, more beautiful, and way more fun.

But there will also be times when questions of efficiency or performance or standardization may come up. Those aren't *bad* questions.

You just don't want the values and logic of mass production or competition to be driving the bus when it comes to discipleship. (Especially if no one even knows you are on a bus, or that *someone* has got to be driving.)

• • •

Summary of Chapter 5: What You See is What You Get

The metaphors we live by shape what seems natural, obvious, or even possible by framing one situation in terms of another. The situational logic that often determines our situational response can be both powerful and automatic.

Any single perspective or lens both highlights and hides important aspects of any given circumstance. If you have more than one lens available to you, you will be able to see more options. You hold different perspectives together in a broader whole, or collage, that informs each of the snapshots.

As you build a more biblical collage, the goal is not merely to change your default way of following Jesus, but to notice your defaults and consider the lens you are using to understand a particular situation. The metaphors you live by will shape what you experience, what you are thinking and feeling, what you consider possible, and what you assume you should do next. Wisdom discerns which lens is an appropriate default to frame the present situation.

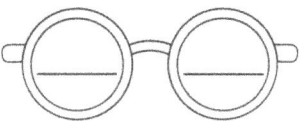

For Further Reflection

If you fell down during a relay race in a competition, what would your feelings tell you about yourself and about other people on your relay team? What actions would seem available to you?

If you tripped and fell during an adventure hiking expedition, what would your feelings tell you about yourself and about other people on your rope team? What actions would seem available to you?

Share a time when you changed your perspective on something. Who was involved? What did you see differently? What made the shift possible?

In what circumstance would it be wise to "look before you leap"? When would it be wise to use a different filter?

Chapter 6

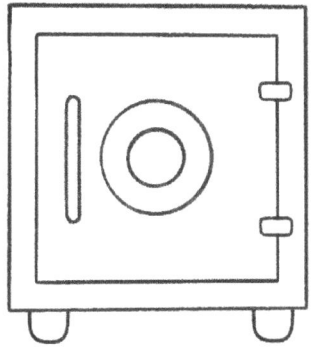 

Bank Vault or Banquet?
Something More than "Outreach"

Our Default Setting: We typically place Jesus at the center of our theology and life together and then experience our faith community as a kind of container with clearly defined boundaries that determine who is "in" and who is "out." We reach *out* to people on the wrong side of the boundary in order to bring them across the boundary and into our group of believers.

Some Good Reasons for Our Default: Reaching new people often involves going to new places. From local service to international mission, we have traditionally labeled that activity "outreach." Outreach seems to fit the Great Commission ("go, and make disciples") and aligns with the typical way we conceive of things that are important as Central. Jesus is naturally IN; outsiders are clearly OUT.

Some Unintended Consequences: The key feature for any "IN-vs-OUT" scenario is the boundary line that defines IN from OUT. No matter what social, moral, or theological features we use to determine that border, the place *insiders* encounter *outsiders* will always be *at the boundary line*. The goal of *out*reach becomes getting people to cross the border from the outside to the inside. Since Jesus is at the center of our life together, outsiders can't be near to Jesus until they cross the boundary lines. "Outreach" can easily

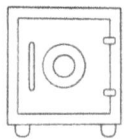

become more about getting people to cross *to our side of the boundary issues* and less about *actually introducing people to Jesus.*

Something More: If you want to shift from Bank Vault assumptions to a Banquet default, reimagine Jesus as moving forward instead of standing still. Don't measure distance from Jesus as much as orientation and movement toward Jesus. Keep Jesus at the *center* of our theology and life together, but also keep Jesus at the *leading edge* of our encounter with outsiders. Reserve judgment on who is "in" and who is "out" and instead focus on helping people take a small next step in the right direction. Recognize your identity "in Christ" and also recognize your role as one who carries "Christ in you." Replace the burden of holding a position of power with the joy of carrying a treasure in ordinary, vulnerable, and accessible jars of clay. Let go of the crucial moment of crossing the boundary to hold onto a lifetime of following Jesus.

• • •

Noticing the "Outreach" Frame

If Jesus told us to "go and make disciples of all nations," then "outreach" seems like the most obvious and natural thing in the world. Where would the Church be if we didn't *pass the faith* to the next generation and *reach out* to new people and bring them *into* the faith?

Back in Chapter 1, we saw how the language of "making" disciples can evoke a production mentality. We can easily get caught up in an assembly line paradigm that actually hinders the work of cultivating Jesus followers. We aren't called to produce a standard model end product called a "disciple;" we are called to the *activity* of "discipling," or "walking with," people from every different and unique background on the planet.

"Outreach" is one of the typical ways we have of talking about the Great Commission to disciple the nations. At times, "discipleship" and "outreach" can even be used synonymously. But we don't merely *talk* that way. We imagine, feel, and reason about, and therefore *live out* the Great Commission

in terms of "reaching" (from our location) "out" to people who don't know Jesus, with the goal of bringing them "in" to our faith or our church.

The uncritical assumptions inherent in the "outreach" paradigm shape what we think we are doing when it comes to introducing new people to Jesus. And, just as we saw with the assembly line, the situational dynamics hidden behind the language of "reaching out" and "bringing in" will predetermine the *obvious* right answers, *natural* outcomes, *clear* dividing lines, and *unquestionable* goals of any evangelistic efforts. The language of "Outreach" is the tip of a cognitive iceberg, a set of sunglasses that filters your perspective, experience, emotions, and actions in some very specific ways.

The Situational Logic of In and Out

Even before babies can talk, human brains learn to recognize patterns in their experience of the physical world. (Books with titles like *Philosophy in the Flesh* and *The Body in the Mind*[1] demonstrate how much our bodies affect our thinking in ways we hardly ever notice or understand.)

One of the earliest patterns we experience is the difference between *In* and *Out*. As we interact with the world around us, the neurons in our brains form pathways we use again and again. Even before we have words for "in" and "out," the polarity of In/Out becomes second nature to us; it's hardwired into our brains at a physical, neural level.[2]

We all use In/Out logic all the time, in a variety of situations, without a second thought. Take this description of a typical morning, for example:

> You wake *out* of a deep sleep and peer *out* from beneath the covers *into* your room. You gradually emerge *out* of your stupor, pull yourself *out* from under the covers, climb *into* your robe, stretch *out* your limbs, and

---

[1] *Philosophy in the Flesh: The Embodied Mind and Its Challenge to Western Thought* (1999) was written by George Lakoff and Mark Johnson (the same two who first published *Metaphors We Live By* in 1980). *Philosophy in the Flesh* builds on Johnson's earlier work, *The Body in the Mind: The Bodily Basis of Meaning, Imagination, and Reason* (1987).

[2] *From Molecule to Metaphor: A Neural Theory of Language* (Jerome A. Feldman, 2006) describes in detail how the Lakoff and Johnson approach to metaphor plays out in the brain at the chemical and molecular level.

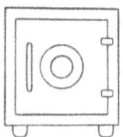

walk *in* a daze *out* of your bedroom and *into* the bathroom. You look *into* the mirror and see your face staring *out* at you. You reach *into* the medicine cabinet, take *out* the toothpaste, squeeze *out* some toothpaste, put the toothbrush *into* your mouth, brush your teeth, and rinse *out* your mouth. At breakfast you perform a host of further *in-out* moves—pouring *out* the coffee, setting *out* the dishes, putting the toast *in* the toaster, spreading *out* the jam on the toast, and on and on.[3]

That conflagration of the literal and non-literal is kind of fun (and a little confusing), but we're not merely playing with language here. Our common ways of *talking* points to common ways of *thinking*—the typical way we imagine and engage the world around us. Our language carries a logic so pervasive in our ordinary experience that we hardly notice it.

The In/Out dichotomy gives rise to one of the most basic building blocks of our conceptual system: the "Container Schema." A few simple but powerful characteristics give shape to our experience of all "container" situations:

- every container has an **interior**;
- every container has an **exterior**;
- every container has **a boundary** that defines the container by distinguishing In from Out.[4]

Based on years of experience, you intuitively know how physical containers work and how to use them in different situations. Containers are good at:

- **keeping separate things separate** (jars of candy in a candy store);
- **protecting what's inside from what's out** (a Ziploc for your ham sandwich; a bank vault for your pearls);
- or **keeping what's inside clean, pure, or undefiled** (the air-tight display case for your Babe Ruth baseball; the tower for Rapunzel).

---

[3] *The Body in the Mind* (Johnson, 1987) quoted in George Lakoff, *Women, Fire, and Dangerous Things: What Categories Reveal about the Mind* (Chicago: University of Chicago Press, 1987), 271.

[4] *Women, Fire, and Dangerous Things* (Lakoff, 1987), 272. Lakoff later refers to the Container source domain as one of the "relatively simple structures that recur in our everyday bodily experience." Lakoff is building on work by Mark Johnson and borrows Johnson's vocabulary of "kinesthetic image-schematic structure," or "image schemas" for short, to label these basic structures inherent in our bodily experience (267).

Who uses containers for these purposes in these different situations? The one who uses the container is usually the one who wants to keep the candy separate, the sandwich fresh, or the souvenir safe.

What could possibly go wrong? The glass jar could break; the Ziploc seal could fail; Rapunzel could let down her hair.

In other words, the boundaries of a container are designed to be crossed, but the primary job of the boundary is to keep IN and OUT separate, and to keep what's on the inside *safe* from what's on the outside.

And what helps a container get its job done? **The appropriate strength and completeness of the boundary becomes the central feature of most any container in most any situation.**

Sometimes a boundary is designed to be porous or semipermeable: a screen door lets in the breeze (but not the bugs). Sometimes a boundary needs to be secure: a screen door on a bank vault (or submarine) would make no sense.

We know, without having to think about it, that the *security* of anything on the inside of a container is directly proportional to *the strength and dependability* of the boundary appropriate for the task at hand.

A Ziploc bag is fine to keep the air away from your sandwich. But a Ziploc with a hole in it is no good: the boundary has been compromised.

Your refrigerator appropriately needs something stronger than a plastic barrier to keep the cold air in and warm air out. But even a refrigerator door isn't strong enough for a submerging submarine.

You put your family pearls in a safe deposit box in a vault at the bank rather than in your refrigerator because the kind of protection your valuables need is different than the kind of protection your ham sandwich needs. Different kinds of boundaries are appropriate for different containers in different situations.

In fact, just as a basic logic flows from the fundamental *structure* of a physical container (you can't simultaneously be IN and OUT), **the *situations* in which we experience containers also come with a set of automatic inferences.**

For example, if the refrigerator door is open, you intuitively know you should close it—not just because Mom said so, but because you know that a

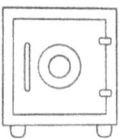

boundary (door) of a container (fridge) must be intact in order to do its job (keep the perishable food safe and preserved).

If you happen to see a *green* jellybean in the *red* jellybean jar, you intuitively know *it doesn't belong there*. You might even be motivated to put that green jellybean back where it belongs, because you know how containers are supposed to work: they keep separate things separate.

Typically, the more *valuable* the contents are, the stronger an appropriate boundary tends to be. While an airtight bank vault *could* protect your ham sandwich, a Ziploc bag will do. (Unless you work in an office where people habitually steal your food; then maybe a padlock on your lunchbox makes sense.) But if your ham on rye were the very first example of the genre, created by Sir John Montagu, the fourth Earl of Sandwich, in 1762, then you would need more than a Ziploc bag. And that airtight display case and humidor may well be kept under lock and key when the museum closes.

So security is one factor. But for an appropriate boundary, *accessibility* also plays a key role: you wouldn't keep your typical Tuesday sandwich in a bank vault even if the vault were air tight, because you can't easily carry a safe around in your lunchbox.

You wouldn't mind making a special trip to the bank to access your grandma's pearls, but the way you normally do lunch on a typical Tuesday means your ham sandwiches need to be much more accessible than that.

Less access = more protection.

For the pearls, that's great. Not so much for the ham sandwich.

The "Container" of Your Faith Community

All of that intuitive knowledge about how physical containers work is a natural part of our conceptual system.[5] We tend to ignore container logic because it functions automatically and unconsciously. As a result, the powerful

---

[5] Some of our basic Western logic going all the way back to Aristotle hinges on what we know intuitively about situations involving containers. See *Philosophy in the Flesh* (Lakoff and Johnson, 1999), 380 ff.

inferences that arise from our knowledge of physical containers usually remain hidden from view. When container logic *obviously* applies to a situation, we get predictable (and seemingly obvious) conclusions and expectations; the container lens goes unnoticed even as it filters our experience.

You automatically reason about *your heart* as a container for your emotions, and you know what it means for your heart to feel small and empty, or large and overflowing. Without conscious thought, you draw conclusions about *your brain* as a container for your ideas, my brain as a container for my ideas, and a book like this one as a way of moving content from one container to another across the boundaries of time and space (and skulls).

Along with your body, heart, and brain, you also experience *social groups* as containers. Your family is a container; your circle of friends is a container; even your country is a kind of container. The dynamics of containers—the purpose, relationship, and expectations of IN, OUT, and the appropriate BOUNDARY between—shape how you perceive and experience the people around you. **Container thinking is just part of the water in which you swim.**

Because you typically, automatically, and uncritically experience social groups as containers, it's not surprising that you naturally experience your faith community as a kind of container, with Jesus at the center.[6] Like all containers, your faith community has an INSIDE, and an OUTSIDE, and an appropriate BOUNDARY between IN and OUT.

For a faith community, the critical "boundary issues" are often *theological*. (My non-denominational friends tell me even non-denoms have certain theological boundary markers; just not a formalized creed or confessional document.) For the denominational container I grew up in, you would have to believe certain things to be on the inside: good and godly things like the

---

[6] Along with In/Out and Up/Down, the opposition Central/Peripheral constitutes a "kinesthetic image schema" which we learn by bodily experience and then apply to non-physical domains. Central is Important is a Conceptual Metaphor ingrained in our way of reasoning about the world (see Lakoff and Johnson, 1999, 380 ff.). Without having to think about it, you know intuitively that Jesus belongs at the Center of Christianity, because he is the most important part.

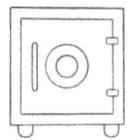

doctrine of the Holy Trinity, the inerrancy of Scripture, a six-day creation, and Jesus' bodily resurrection on the third day, to name just a few.

For any faith community, *social issues* become another kind of identifying boundary: if you grew up in a denominational container like mine, people naturally assume you share a Pro-Life and Anti-Gay Marriage political agenda (at least in the American Midwest "container," which I also inhabit).

And then there is the Moral Barrier: certain *immoral behavior* is evidence you are on the outside of the community, behavior like cohabitation before marriage or even voting for the wrong political party.

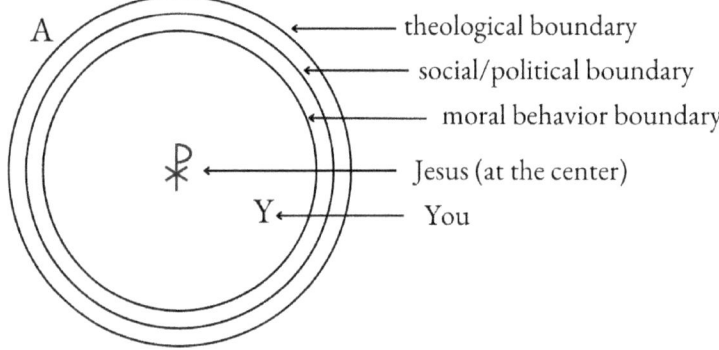

No matter how your group defines the boundary of your denomination or faith community—as a theological confession, a list of social issues, or a moral code—**the boundary itself is the most important feature of any container.**

And the automatic reasoning inherent in your experience of containers gets uncritically applied to your faith community.

Theological, social, and moral barriers are "obviously" designed to:

- keep separate things separate;
- keep things on the inside safe or protected;
- keep what is inside clean, pure, or undefiled.

It's also "obvious" that **the appropriate strength of the boundary is directly related to the value of what's inside.** And since your faith (or even your *Jesus*) is as valuable as it gets, it's easy to assume that the appropriate boundaries should be as strong as possible (even if more protection = less access). A Ziploc bag for the Gospel just will not do.

Because you already know that for any given container (A), any object (X) is either IN or OUT of the container, you "know" that all the people in your life are either IN or OUT of the Christian container of your faith. It's also obvious that if object (X) is in container (B), and container (B) is *not* inside a second container, container (A), then object (X) is also *not* in container (A).

It sounds confusing when you try to make a mathematical formula out of it, but that reasoning is actually as simple as knowing that the sandwich in your lunchbox is *not* in the refrigerator as long as your lunchbox is *on the kitchen counter*. You don't have to do the math; the conclusion is self-evident.

container A (your faith community)

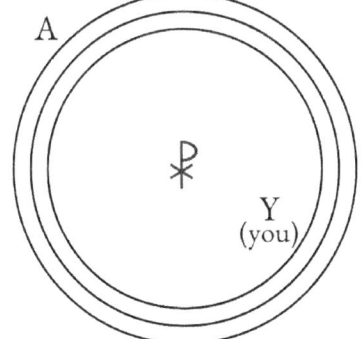

container B (the pagan world)

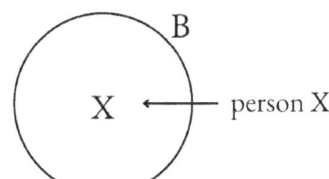

(someone who doesn't already share the theology, social agenda, or morality of your church)

In the same way, you don't need to think about it to know that a person in the *Mormon*, or *Hindu*, or *Buddhist* container is *not* in the *Christian* container; those World Religion containers seem mutually exclusive. In fact, *anyone* outside the theological, social/political, or moral boundaries of your faith container will, *by definition*, seem to belong outside the community.

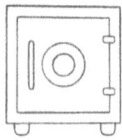

The Central Role of the Boundary in Outreach

The *boundary* serves as *the defining feature* of any container. The boundary's job is to separate the interior from the exterior. Therefore, **the boundary defines what it means to be IN or OUT.**

In practical terms, you will naturally check the boundary to determine your status of IN or OUT. Are you still in the US, or have you drifted into Canada? Find where you are *in relationship to the border*, and you automatically know. Are you a "good Christian?" Are you even *saved*? The Container lens leads you to consult the boundary issues of your local faith community.

You naturally know whether you are IN or OUT by your relationship to the theological, social/political, and moral behavior standards of your community. As long as you are on the right side of those boundary issues, your mind will automatically reason that you are IN, and your emotions will affirm a sense of security and belonging.

If you are living or believing outside of the boundary issues of your local faith community, your mind will automatically reason that you are OUT, and your emotions will tell you that you are not welcome, you aren't safe, and you don't belong *in here* with all these good, religious people.

Because *Jesus* is the most important thing in your life of faith, Jesus is clearly at the center. But if you want to know whether *you* are IN or OUT—if you want to know if you are *saved* or not—you don't look to the CENTER.

If you are reasoning from within a Container mindset, you automatically look to the BOUNDARY to see if you are IN or OUT.

So instead of looking to *Jesus* when you question your faith or your salvation, the Container lens naturally leads you to look at all the theological, social/political, and moral behavior markers your faith community uses to define IN from OUT. In this way, Christianity becomes a religion of the Law: without trying to, or even meaning to, you replace trust in Jesus with a list of doctrines, political opinions, and moral do's and don'ts. And you will feel either comfort or despair depending on how well you think you line up with those boundary issues.

You also consult the boundary lines (not the center) to see if *other people* are IN or OUT. It is the most natural thing in the world to "know," without having to think about it, whether or not people belong *in* the Christian container (and therefore if they should have *access* to Jesus).

That guy cusses too much; he *clearly* doesn't belong around here. That woman is an Arab; she *couldn't* be interested in Jesus. Those people voted for the wrong political candidate; they must not be *real* Christians.

These kinds of conclusions are obvious, natural, and automatic. The logic doesn't need to consider Jesus at all in the equation: the CENTER might tell you what's important, but the BOUNDARY determines what's IN or OUT.

I'm not saying we *should* reason this way. I'm not saying we *try* to reason this way. I'm just saying, *without trying,* this is the way we automatically and unconsciously reason about our own status and the status of others. It's part of the water we have trouble seeing because we are swimming in it all the time.

You intuitively know, without stopping to think about it, that **you have to cross the container's boundary to get from OUT to IN.**

The same holds true for your faith community: to go from *outside* the Church to *inside* the Church, it seems obvious that you have to cross the key boundaries set up as identifying markers by the local faith community.

Those identity markers will tend to be social, political, doctrinal, and behavioral, without any necessary reference to the person of Jesus.

The specifics of those boundaries will change depending on where in the world and when in history you live. Nonetheless, those boundary issues, whatever they are, become the most defining features of your faith container.

It seems *natural and intuitive* for people in my theological container, for example, to feel like we have to get outsiders to assent to a six-day creation and an inerrant scripture, change all their incorrect political views, and give up their immoral lifestyle *before* we could possibly introduce them to the Jesus at the center of our faith (even though, in a different context, we would also say that Jesus is the only one who can forgive sins and transform lives).

Your local faith community might have different theological, political, or moral behavior boundary markers than mine does, but all containers work the

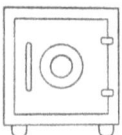

same. Our **container mentality naturally and automatically places *Jesus* and *outsiders* as far away[7] from each other as possible.**

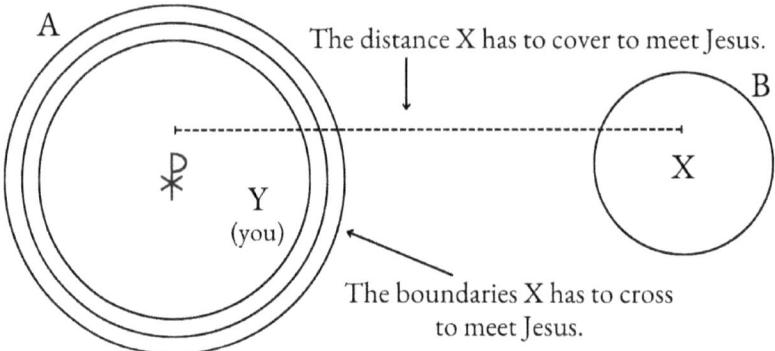

In terms of outreach and evangelism, it becomes obvious and natural that, once you have gone all the way OUT to where those unbelievers are, you then have to bring them all the way back, across all of the boundary issues, before they can be near Jesus. **"Outreach" by default begins to focus on getting people to cross the theological, social, and moral behavior boundaries that define IN from OUT** rather than introducing people to Jesus or sharing Good News. I mean, the ultimate point is Good News; but you have to cross the boundaries first!

To be fair, you can find multiple examples of a Container mindset in the teachings of Jesus, where a clear boundary distinguishes IN from OUT. However—and this is a big *however*—the IN/OUT teachings of Jesus are specifically *not* about outreach. Rather, these parables *concern the Last Day*.[8]

---

[7] "Relational Distance is Physical Distance" is another one of the "kinesthetic image-schematic structures" that allow us to reason about non-physical experiences (like relationships) in terms of physical experience (like physical distance between two objects).

[8] The Parable of the Wheat and Tares (Matthew 13:24-30), the Parable of the Fishing Net (Matthew 13:47-50), the Parable of the Ten Virgins (Matthew 25:1-13), the Parable of the Talents (Matthew 25:14-30), and the Sheep and the Goats (Matthew 25:31-46), for example, all utilize IN/OUT dynamics, and all are teachings about the End Times. Jesus himself seems to reserve the IN/OUT dichotomy for eschatology, not missiology (or even ecclesiology).

When Jesus encounters real people—as he walks and eats and teaches and prays and visits homes and celebrates religious festivals—we *don't* see Jesus setting up moral, social, or even theological boundaries people have to cross in order to get access to him. In fact, you see just the opposite.

Jesus at the Center and at the Leading Edge

If Central is Important, then Jesus certainly belongs at the center of our faith, since Jesus is the most important thing about Christianity. But the Center is as far away as you can get from the Outside (and the outsiders who live there)!

The way the New Testament talks, there are no boundaries outsiders have to cross *before* they get access to Jesus. Following Jesus doesn't come with a list of prerequisites. **We constantly find Jesus crossing all kinds of moral, social, and theological boundaries in order to meet people right where they live.**

You could even characterize Jesus' mission as *living on the border*: Jesus lives on the border of heaven and earth, divine and human, promise and fulfillment. But he also quite literally spends significant amounts of time in geographical borderlands or with people who are marginal or marginalized.[9]

So Jesus seems to upset our default understanding of how IN and OUT should work for our faith Container. Jesus doesn't remain safely in the Center. How else might we think about who, and *where,* Jesus is in our life of faith? Jesus himself points the way. Teaching about the Good Shepherd, Jesus says:

> I am *the gate;* whoever enters through me will be saved. They will come in and go out, and find pasture.
>
> John 10:9 (NIV)

A few chapters later, just before heading to the Garden of Gethsemane, Jesus tells his disciples that he is going away to prepare a place for them, but that they already know the way to the place he is going. Thomas is bold enough to say, "We don't know the place, so how can we know the way?"

---

[9] See Leopoldo A. Sánchez M., *Sculptor Spirit: Models of Sanctification from Spirit Christology* (2019), esp. Chapter 6, "Welcoming the Stranger: The Hospitality Model."

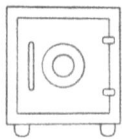

The response Jesus gives uses our experience of locations as Containers to talk about our relational status with the Heavenly Father:

> I am *the way* and the truth and the life. No one comes to the Father except *through* me.
>
> John 14:6 (NIV)

If Jesus is the Gate, or the Door, or the Way Through, then maybe we can reset the default on how our faith container works. If you want get at your sandwich, you open the Ziploc bag; if someone rings your doorbell, you open the front door to talk to them. **The Opening or Access Point or Door is the place on the boundary where Outsiders and Insiders encounter each other.**

Jesus can still be at the Center of our faith (though the way he talks in John, Jesus himself might put *the Father* at the Center). But seeing Jesus as the Access Point or Door makes **Jesus the place where Outsiders meet Insiders.** That seems like a big improvement to me.

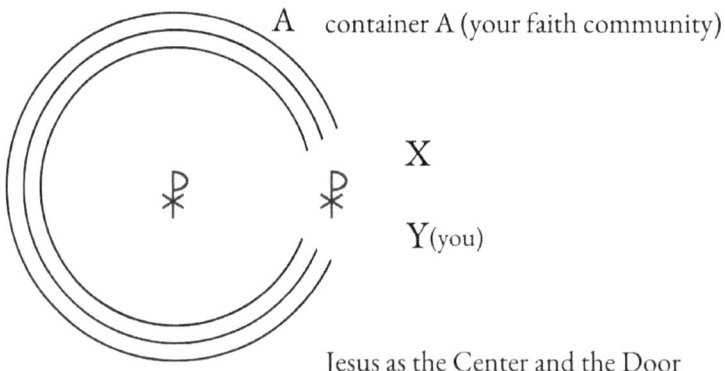

Jesus as the Center and the Door

Instead of getting Outsiders to adopt a theological position on an inspired, inerrant Scripture, you introduce them to Jesus.

Instead of confronting Outsiders with all the reasons they should vote the way you do, you introduce them to Jesus.

Instead of trying to police behavior or demonstrate moral superiority, you introduce people to Jesus. Jesus is the one who can change hearts and lives. Jesus can bring Outsiders into the presence of the Father.

And if an Outsider doesn't respond immediately, at least they have brushed elbows *with Jesus,* instead of only bumping up against your theological, political, or moral boundary issues (as far away from Jesus as possible).

Keeping Jesus as the Gate or Access Point means **you define IN and OUT with reference to *Jesus*, not in reference to the Boundary.** If you want to know your status, you wouldn't immediately check your morals or your politics; you would look to *Jesus.* **Jesus is the Way In.**

But **Jesus is also the Way Out.** Notice how the Gate works: the sheep will *come in and go out* and find pasture (John 10:14).

For sheep, all the good stuff they need to thrive is not contained inside the sheepfold. Their paddock is safe, yet they must leave the sheepfold in order to survive. That's why they need a Good Shepherd. They listen to his voice, and the Good Shepherd both protects and leads the sheep.

That important inference—*that the good stuff we need for abundant life is outside the sheep pen*—reverses our bank vault default. Instead of the good stuff being well protected on the Inside, the good stuff is on the Outside. We still need a way to be safe, but safe *on the Outside* (pasture) as well as safe on the Inside (sheep pen), and safe all along the Way.

The Shepherd and Sheep lens adds a sense of Journey or Movement to the Container mindset. Jesus is the Gate who provides a Way In (and Out), as well as the Good Shepherd, who leads the sheep to pasture so they can have abundant life. The social group as Flock is no longer a *static* Container, like a bank vault. The Flock is by necessity a Container *on the move.*

When you put the Container in motion, a few important things happen. First, **your position in relationship to Jesus is reckoned by orientation,** not just distance. In other words, if Jesus is on the move, and you stay in the same place, you can conclude without thinking about it that the distance between Jesus and you will increase over time. Your job description as a Sheep is to listen to the Shepherd's voice and to follow; orientation and movement

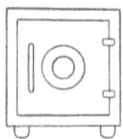

suddenly become important, and that aligns with the central job description of a disciple: to follow your master.

Secondly, **your relationship to Outsiders also becomes dynamic.** If you (Y) and someone you disagree with (person X) are both oriented toward Jesus and following where he leads, the two of you will get closer to each other, *not by focusing on boundary issues,* but by focusing on Jesus.

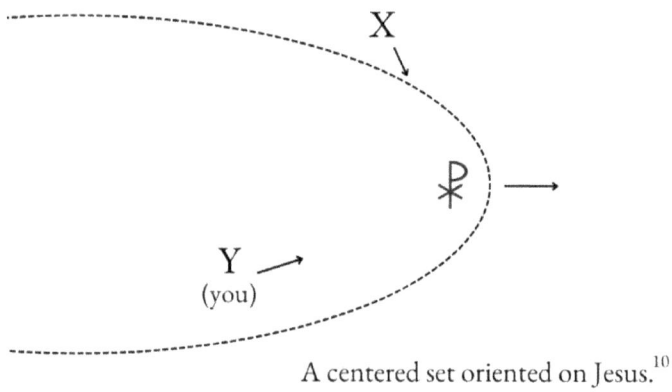

A centered set oriented on Jesus.[10]

Finally, **the location of your faith experience changes.** You don't look for religious activity only *inside* your church building container. You don't expect Jesus to show up only on Sunday mornings. You don't wait for outsiders to come into the secure bank vault of your faith community to meet Jesus; you are free to encounter both Jesus and outsiders *outside* in the real world.

Jesus becomes not only the most important (central) thing about your faith; Jesus is also at the leading edge of your faith community, leading you out where abundant life can be had. (And also keeping you safe—indeed, laying down his life—because it can be dangerous outside the pen.)

---

[10] *Missional Church: A Vision for the Sending of the Church in North America,* ed. Darrell L. Guder (1998) uses a similar diagram on page 210, although theirs includes both the "Covenant Community" as a bounded set and the "Congregation" as a centered set. The "Pilgrim People of God" or "Mission Community" overlaps parts of both the Covenant Community and the Mission Community in Guder's illustration. I like the distinction between a bounded set (defined by the boundary) and a centered set (defined by orientation toward and relationship to the center), and the sense of movement Guder gives to the Reign of God.

Reframing your faith Container as a *flock*, with Jesus at the leading edge, flips the script on mission. Instead of an institution that *sends people out*, the Church becomes a fellowship of *those who are sent out;* or perhaps better, *those who are led out*, and therefore as those who are never without the presence, guidance, and protection of their Shepherd.

If the Church is a Flock, following our Good Shepherd, then the "good stuff" doesn't just happen on Sunday morning in the church building. In fact, Flock reasoning leads us to expect that *only in the going out,* only in the missional life of the Church out in the world, will we truly find the abundant life our Good Shepherd intends.

Sheep locked in a bank vault will die. And while you could theoretically keep them alive, and safe, in that secure crypt, sheep were never meant to thrive in a bank vault. The Good Shepherd brings them in, *and leads them out*, and calls them by name, and gives them abundant life.

Sharing the Gospel as Hospitality

Container thinking isn't all bad. But framing your faith community primarily as a kind of bank vault can make at least one important inference feel natural and obvious: that people *not like me* must first become *more like me* before I can introduce them to Jesus.

I'm not sure we could get rid of IN and OUT thinking entirely, even if we wanted to, since Container logic is hardwired into the neurocircuitry of our brains. **But as long as Bank Vault thinking is the only way we process the Container dynamics of "outreach," our default actions and attitudes will all involve keeping distance and strong barriers between Jesus and outsiders.**

Maybe we can reframe Container thinking and reimagine our role. Flock thinking is a good start; it puts the Container in motion and places Jesus at the leading edge of our encounter with outsiders. If the good stuff like green pastures and quiet waters are on the outside of the sheep pen, then maybe the Church could function less like a *bank vault* and more like a movable feast, a

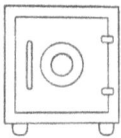

banquet out there, where the outsiders are; a banquet that combines hospitality with the Kingdom of God.

A careful look at the Gospels shows us that Jesus spends a lot of time either attending or teaching about banquets—or even both at the same time! If Jesus is teaching about the coming End Times Feast, the future Great Wedding Banquet of the Lamb (as Revelation calls it), then the division between IN and OUT couldn't be more stark.[11]

In the meantime, in the *now* time, **Jesus lives in a way that assumes his very presence breaks down barriers and brings outsiders into the presence of God.** In Luke 14, for example, Jesus is at a *banquet* as he teaches one of his *banquet parables.* (The whole scene feels a bit like the movie *Inception*; you sometimes can't tell where the parable stops and real life begins.)

The rich people in the parable RSVP yes to a banquet invitation, just like the rich people at the actual table with Jesus. But once the animals have been taken out of the flock and put on the buffet line, and the messenger tells the guests that dinner is served, these social elites in the parable all come up with the most outrageous excuses for not showing up. They have conspired together to shame the host.

The host's anger gets expressed in mercy when he sends a messenger with an invitation to gather the kinds of people that would ruin most ritually clean dinner parties: the blind, and lame, and crippled, and those who would, by virtue of their presence, contaminate good religious people and make them unfit for religious service. And when even that generous act leaves room at the table, the messenger of the invitation is sent out where the Outsiders live—way out to the foreigners, and outcasts, and actively contagious.

"Compel them to come in!" the Master orders (Luke 14:23). But, contra the way the Spanish Inquisition read that verse, this *compelling* has to do with overcoming their legitimate objections: I can't pay you back! I don't belong

---

[11] Recall that, while the IN/OUT division may be stark on the Last Day, that stark division is also reserved *for the Last Day*. You can't cull the bad fish from the good fish before the net is dragged to shore. You can't separate the sheep and the goats before the Final Judgement. You can't remove the weeds from the wheat ahead of time. In fact, the according to the Parable of the Wheat and the Tares, *you can't even tell the weeds from the wheat* until the harvest.

here! You don't want somebody like me around! If you touch me, you will be unclean! You must mean someone else!

That banquet parable has a Center and Periphery. You still have a movement from Outside to Inside by means of crossing a Boundary. But look *how* that Boundary gets crossed! The Messenger of the Invitation is sent from Inside to Out, across the Boundary, and compels people who know they don't deserve it and can't repay it, to enter into the presence of the host and sit at banquet. While Jesus may be the host of the End Times Banquet, his ministry also embodies the Messenger of the Invitation.

Theologically, what Jesus is doing counts as bringing Outsiders across religious, ethnic, and socio-economic boundaries IN to the center to give them a seat at the table. What that looks like *in practice,* before the End Times Banquet, is very different. Jesus himself is often the *guest* at any given dinner party. And when Jesus sits down as guest at a table full of outcasts and outsiders, he ends up bringing the Center, the Eternal Banquet, the Presence of the Almighty God, with him to the feast.

In the inverted logic of the Gospel, **Jesus lives out his ministry as an outsider who needs welcome, so that he can bring the Kingdom Banquet to those very outsiders who will welcome him in.**

Jesus is born in extremely marginal circumstances—his pregnant, teenage mom was engaged to some guy who wasn't the father. Sketchy at best. After the Magi visit, Jesus and his family escape Herod by fleeing to Egypt; they were political refugees in a foreign country. Jesus grew up a child of immigrants.

When they finally do return home, Jesus and his family settle in Galilee, on purpose. Galilee is far from the center of political, economic, and religious power in Jerusalem—so far, in fact, that the region was known as "Galilee of the Gentiles," a place where you could hardly tell a Jew from all the unclean, alien outsiders around them.

Did you know Galileans had a peculiar accent? They didn't sound like the people at the Center; they were definitely Outsiders. If Jesus didn't still have an Egyptian accent when he grew up, he probably spoke a lot like Peter, James, and John. And remember, Peter's Galilean *accent* gives him away to the

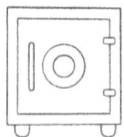

servants and bystanders in the High Priest's courtyard (Matthew 26:73). Even *the help* speak better than those outsider Galileans! Leopoldo Sánchez summarizes it well: "Jesus knows what it's like to be a vulnerable outsider."[12]

Jesus didn't do "outreach" the way we imagine it. He didn't invite his neighbors to church on Easter. Once he started his public ministry, Jesus didn't even have a house where he could throw a party and invite some outsiders over for dinner. The Temple was his Father's house, and Jesus went *out* from there, dependent on the welcome of other people, often outsiders. And, anointed with the Spirit of God, Jesus took the presence of the Father into the homes of outsiders who welcomed him in.

Think again of the Samaritan woman at the well. Although she is going to draw water at noon (her personal history has made her an outcast), it's still her people, her town, her well. *Jesus* is the outsider. And when he asks, in that accent that sounded too Samaritan to good Jews but would have been far too Jewish for this Samaritan woman, Jesus doesn't invite her to the banquet. Instead, he asks her for a drink.

She certainly knows that receiving food from a Samaritan's hand would be defiling for a Jew (there's that boundary again), but with Jesus, contamination works in reverse. **Wherever Jesus goes is the center.** Whomever Jesus touches becomes clean. And by taking on the role of Guest, Jesus is simultaneously acting as Messenger of the Invitation, and inviting this woman, whom he asks for a drink, to receive from him living water that wells up to eternal life.

The role of Messenger of the Invitation is contagious; the woman at the well goes back to her own people, the ones who had made her a social outcast, and she invites them to come and see a man who *certainly can't be* the Christ. (But what if he is?) By accepting her invitation, the whole village comes out to meet Jesus and in turn become hosts: they invite Jesus and his disciples into their village, to stay with them for three days. (But where would they sleep? Bedding down under a Samaritan roof would make good Jews unclean. It

---

[12] Sánchez, *Sculptor Spirit* (2019), 145. Sánchez goes on to cite Virgilio Elizondo's "Galilee principle," to talk about both the ministry of Jesus and those Jesus chooses to commission for work in the Kingdom: "what humans reject, God chooses as his very own."

seems the presence of Jesus reverses the contamination, so these foreign homes become mini-temples, housing the very presence of God in Jesus.)

Jesus is constantly putting himself in the role of dinner guest, so that he can bring the Eternal Banquet to the table. Jesus tells the outsider, tax collector, Roman sympathizer, vertically challenged Zacchaeus *not,* "You should come over to my house for dinner," *but rather:* "Zacchaeus, come down from that tree; it is necessary for me to come to *your* house today" (Luke 19:5). *Zacchaeus* is the host. *Jesus* is the guest. And yet, by being the guest, Jesus is able to bring *salvation* to the table, as his dish to pass (Luke 19:9).

This *being-a-guest-for-the-sake-of-bringing-salvation* was so typical of Jesus the haters regularly accused him of "eating with sinners." Their concern: eat with people like that and they'll never change their outsider living. Eat with people like that and they'll never recognize the boundaries! Eat with people like that and you could get contaminated!

That's the Boundary thinking at the heart of the familiar parable of the Good Samaritan (Luke 10). When the priest and Levite pass the beaten man dying in the ditch, *they have good reason*: they are on their way to do something important and holy.

If that's a dead body on the side of the road (and if it's not right this second, it's about to become one), then touching a corpse brings a contamination with a cool down period; you would have to wash and then wait until the next day until you were clean again. But if you had important Temple things to be about today, you couldn't afford to take the day off for Corpse Decontamination. These good, religious people have good, religious duties, and good Container Boundary reasons for not getting involved.

It's the Outsider Samaritan who plays the role of host in the parable: the hated foreigner takes the beaten Jew out of the ditch, tends his wounds, gets him to safety, and covers the cost of his convalescence.

Is Jesus supposed to be the Good Samaritan in the story? Maybe. He is sometimes the host. But in his typical practice, **Jesus usually becomes *the host* by becoming *the guest* first**. In this case, that would mean *Jesus* is the Jewish

man naked and bleeding in the ditch. (Wait a few chapters in Luke and we will indeed see Jesus naked and bleeding on the cross.)

The Samaritan receives Jesus in, with, and under the guise of an Outsider in need. And by being the gracious host, or good neighbor, the Samaritan receives the One who brings salvation to his house.

The tradition of receiving God in the guise of the foreigner has strong Old Testament ties. Father Abraham, after all, once welcomed three strangers into his home and discovered only afterward that they were Messengers of the Invitation (Genesis 18). Jesus became human, even a naked and bleeding human, so that he could *need hospitality*; so that, in the act of receiving hospitality, Jesus might become both Invitation and Host.

Jesus, who alone can offer eternal help, becomes *one who needs help*, so that, by receiving help, he can deliver the help only he can give.

We are called to that kind of upside down ministry. We are at our best as a church, not in our strength, but in our vulnerability. Oh, we should feed the hungry and clothe the naked and welcome in the outsider: teaching on the Sheep and Goats, Jesus says, "In as much as you have done this to the least of my brothers, you have done it unto me" (Matthew 25:40). To feed, clothe, visit, pray for, and welcome the marginal and marginalized *is* to receive Jesus.

But the dynamic goes even further. Just as Jesus became weak, and vulnerable, and marginal, and marginalized so that he could bring salvation to those who welcome him in, so you are sent outside the normal boundaries of your routine, outside your comfort zone, outside to where all the outsiders are, not in strength, but as weak, and vulnerable, and marginal, and marginalized.

You are the Samaritan woman at the well. You are the Galilean fisherman. You carry the presence of Jesus with you, in Ziploc bags. And whoever welcomes *you*, Jesus says, is actually welcoming *him* (John 13:20).

When we imagine "outreach," we typically think of ourselves at the Center, with Jesus. From that position of strength, we are able to "reach out" to help the outsiders. *Theologically*, from the perspective of the Last Day, that is indeed what's actually going on. What that looks like *in practice*, before the End Times Banquet, is very different.

As one baptized into Christ and filled with the Spirit, you carry the Center, the Eternal Banquet, the Presence of the Almighty God, with you, out to where the outsiders live. In your vulnerability and weakness, in your need, you will be welcomed by people you might consider outsiders.

But pay attention! Jesus may be putting you in a place of desperate need so that he can bring the Kingdom Banquet to those outsiders who welcome you in. "Anyone who receives you, receives me," Jesus said. "And anyone who receives me receives the One who sent me" (Matthew 10:40).

If all we have is Bank Vault mentality, then we need the Boundaries to be strong so that we feel safe on the Inside with Jesus. We will go Out from a position of strength with the intention of helping people (out there) who are in need, with the hope that eventually, we can get them to cross all of our Boundary issues so that they can be on the Inside with us (and with Jesus).

But if we can reframe outreach in terms of Banquet, then maybe we can imagine taking Jesus with us, *out* into the world. Maybe we don't have to be strong or powerful all the time. Maybe the places we feel most vulnerable and most in need are places where Outsiders will welcome *us* in. It's not fun to be the one who needs help. But as they receive you, they also receive the One who sends you.

Jesus lived as a marginal character: he was a child refugee, grew up in a backwater part of the country, and was constantly inviting himself over to other people's houses for dinner, because he had no house (or dinner) of his own.[13]

Jesus welcomed marginal characters, and then used those same marginal characters to bring an invitation to others. Jesus sent a healed demoniac back to his Gentile friends and family with good news; he sent an outcast Samaritan woman back into her Samaritan village with a startling message; he sent some Galilean fishermen, with accents that made them sound uneducated, to refined religious experts and smooth-talking intellectuals.

---

[13] At times in his itinerant ministry Jesus did have people caring for his needs. He was certainly welcome in the house of Mary, Martha, and Lazarus, for example. But Jesus sums up the standard procedure for the traveling preacher: "Foxes have dens and birds have nests, but the Son of Man has no place to lay his head" (Matthew 8:20; Luke 9:58).

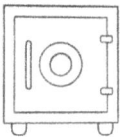

That marginal Jesus, whose mission is so often to and through marginal people, is the Jesus being shaped in you. The Spirit shapes you to be a person on the margins, with one foot in the resurrection of the dead and life of the world to come, and one foot in a broken and hurting world.

The Spirit shapes your heart to welcome people on the margins who don't share your economic status, your way of talking, or your political views. And when you find yourself on the outside of a social group, when you experience weakness and vulnerability on the margins, the Spirit shapes in you the Jesus who humbled himself so much that he didn't always know where his next meal was coming from or where he would find shelter for the night—the Jesus who humbled himself so he could be received by people on the margins, and that by receiving him, they might be part of the banquet feast of God.

Bank Vault thinking teaches you fear. You *naturally* assume you should be afraid of people on the other side of all those boundary issues. The Center is *obviously* the place of security, importance, and power. And, if you live at the Center, you will quite *logically* be terrified of being displaced.

But when you encounter people on the margins—even when you are marginalized—you carry with you the Center, the Power, the *Jesus* who is Guest, and Host, and Life of every party he attends.

You have this treasure in jars of clay, because you can't carry a bank vault with you to all the places Jesus wants to send you next. You have this treasure in jars of clay so the people you meet at the margins will have access to this treasure where they need it most, right in the middle of their ordinary lives. [14]

• • •

---

[14] Jesus is not only IN the Container of the Church, he can also be IN the Container of the individual believer. At the same time, the individual believer can also be IN Christ. When the focus is on *identity*, you can trust that *you are the treasure* and your Identity in Christ is Fort Knox. You are sheltered. You are protected. You are secure. Your salvation depends on it. But when *Jesus is the treasure*, then your job is to be an ordinary, on the move, portable, and vulnerable Container. "We have this treasure in jars of clay," (2 Corinthians 4:7) so that the treasure in you is *accessible* to those around you. *Their* salvation depends on it. For a nuanced reading of the Container Schema in a NT text, see Bonnie Howe's commentary *Because You Bear This Name: Conceptual Metaphor and the Moral Meaning of 1 Peter*.

Summary of Chapter 6: Bank Vault or Banquet?

When it comes to reasoning about and experiencing our life together in the world, we have options. Our automatic default position, although it feels natural and obvious, is perhaps the worst option in front of us. When we unthinkingly frame ourselves *Inside* a social group Container and then see the Boundary as the defining feature of our faith group, we miss some of the most important aspects of our Christian life in the world.

There is no single correct way of imagining the Church that should supplant this Bank Vault mentality. But whatever we do, we should stop using our boundary issues as the central defining feature of the local faith community. Such an *uncritical*, *natural*, and seemingly *obvious* approach points *believers* away from Jesus and to the boundary markers to find their identity; and it points *unbelievers* away from Jesus and to the boundary markers as the essence of what it means to be Christian. We should stop that.

But what do we do instead? The Scriptures certainly use Container imagery to talk about our life of faith. Use that imagery wisely and carefully. Don't bring the clear IN/OUT polarity of the Last Day into our present interaction with the world. Let the wheat and tares grow together; the angels will be able to tell them apart at the harvest.

Comfort people with the strength of their identity IN Christ, but also call them to living life as a vulnerable vessel (like Jesus did) so the treasure of the Gospel IN them can be accessible to regular people in their ordinary workweek.

Keep Jesus as the most important (and Central) thing in your life of faith, but also look for Jesus at the leading edge of our encounter with outsiders. Notice when your emotions or your default lenses make it natural for you to want to keep away from outsiders; look instead for the invitation of Jesus, "Follow me!" and the promise of Jesus, "Whoever receives you, receives me."

Play with new ways of framing the church's life in the world. Try out the Hospitality lens as a way of imagining how you live as a congregation or a family. Run some small experiments in treating faith more like a Banquet and less like a Bank Vault, more like a Block Party and less like a Blockade. Rub elbows with some Outsiders as if you carried treasure in jars of clay.

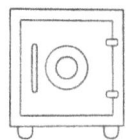

You may feel pressure to "get it right." Trade that pressure in for a deeper dependence on Jesus, who has got you covered, even when you get it wrong. Try something—anything—different than placing all of your social, political, moral, and theological boundaries between Jesus and people who don't yet know Jesus. Invite them to follow and, over time—as you keep following, too—you will find you are moving closer together. Don't give up your theology; just don't make your theology a barrier to meeting Jesus.

If all that feels like a kind of a big deal, you're not wrong. Even noticing, let alone actually rewiring, *what goes without saying* is a real challenge. But wow! What a difference, to live as if you get to carry Jesus into the world without having to police the lives of unbelievers! What a relief to see, not just your strength or your generosity or your benevolence, but your *weakness* and your *need* as the playground of God's Kingdom activity in Jesus!

If Jesus is calling us away from Bank Vault and toward Banquet living (like I truly believe he is), then Jesus will also supply his Spirit for the work and the adventure that such a change will bring.

Come, Holy Spirit, and shape Jesus in us!

This Changes Everything

	The Bank Vault	The Banquet
Jesus	The valuable treasure we keep safe and locked away.	The host and the guest; the Life of the party.
The Church	The container defined by moral, ethical, and theological boundaries; the people "inside."	A movable feast, grounded in life together, where there is always room for one more at the table.
The World	"Outsiders" who pose a threat to the content of the container.	People who get an invitation. People who host us in our need.
The Goal	Protect what's on the inside from what's on the outside. Keep the defining lines strong and clear. Make sure the boundary is intact.	Offer hospitality to the last and the least. Receive hospitality from people not like me. Look for Jesus at work in both.
My Role	Reinforce the boundaries whenever possible. Make sure I am on the right side of all the boundary issues. Protect our faith from contamination by our culture.	I am welcomed by Jesus, and I welcome others on behalf of Jesus. I enjoy the feast and I enjoy bringing the invitation. Jesus works in my weakness. I wonder what will happen next!
Key Thinking	Jesus is at the center of our faith. Our faith is best protected by strengthening moral, ethical, and theological boundaries. Only people affirming boundary issues can be allowed to get to the center.	I don't deserve a place at the table, yet I love being at the party! I look for Jesus at the center of my faith and at the leading edge of my encounter with "outsiders."

For Further Reflection

Noticing Container dynamics in your everyday thinking and acting can be a challenge: the distinction between In and Out seems natural and obvious.

Take some time to notice ways you daily interact with your body, your relationships, or your environment in terms of In, Out, and crossing a Boundary. Make a list, below.

Once you have a dozen or so items on your list, compare notes with a friend.

Container dynamics can cause automatic and uncritical *emotional* responses. It just *feels* wrong to have one red M&M in the green M&M jar; you might move it (or eat it) without really thinking about it.

When your boundary lines are challenged, you want to protect what's Inside; so you will naturally *feel* threatened.

One study I once read showed that people are way more likely to swallow their own saliva if it stays in their mouth than if the saliva is first spit into a glass. It's the same spit, but once it crosses the threshold of the body, we feel a *natural revulsion* to letting it back in.

How do those natural feelings of *that doesn't belong here*, or *that's threatening me*, or even, *that's disgusting!* complicate our interaction with other people?

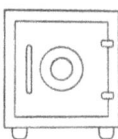

What kinds of feelings belong to a banquet setting? How would those feelings lead us to treat other people?

Share a story about a time when you were weak or vulnerable and Jesus used that situation to bless you and bless someone who welcomed you.

Chapter 7

Pitched Battle or Pitched Tent?
Something More than "Defending the Faith"

Our Default Setting: We typically frame opposing worldviews in terms of warfare. Without trying to or meaning to, we feel like everything said against our faith is a kind of attack. We experience outsiders as enemies. We defend the truth of God's Word, often by launching a counterattack. We naturally assume that we can only win or lose this battle, and eternal life is at stake.

Some Good Reasons for Our Default: We really don't agree on some pretty important issues, and because Truth is involved, issues often feel very black and white. The culture we live in reinforces a natural tendency to respond to any kind of conflict or disagreement by going into defense (or attack) mode.

Some Unintended Consequences: Christians can end up feeling under attack most of the time. Anger, fear, avoidance, and verbal counterattacks are all natural, obvious, and reasonable responses. The mandate to win any given argument is so urgent and powerful, and the stakes are so high, that Christians end up acting in ways that don't seem very Christ-like; but warfare requires behavior that would not be acceptable in other settings. That's just how war works. Conflict can even be exhilarating. And constant conflict is exhausting.

Something More: Recognize the Warfare default setting; then expand your options. Think of argument as a kind of dance, where both partners are working together for the mutual benefit of both. Frame dissonance and tension in terms

of music or gardening: as natural and necessary for movement and growth. Most of all, see Jesus as *God with us*, the portable Tent of God's presence in the midst of a wandering people. View outsiders as people who offer and receive hospitality. Preserve a place for the experience of enemies in your theological collage, but prioritize ways you can spend unhurried time with people not like you. Slow down and enjoy the people God puts in front of you. Trust that Jesus is present in your *being with*.

• • •

Argument is War

Because our way of seeing and inhabiting the world *just feels right*, even describing that default setting can seem like an attack. Fish tend to get defensive about their water...

I want to talk about how we naturally tend to get defensive as individual Christians and as the Church. But if I start there, you could reasonably feel like you or your local congregation are under fire. Your natural reaction would be to defend yourself and fight back. You could attack my writing, or my logic, or even me as an author or person (fight); or you could put this stupid book down and never read it again (flight). Either way, you have the power to win this argument (since I am not there to defend myself).

So let's not start there. Let's see how Argument is War works in a different setting before we try to notice our own Christian defaults. Let's flip the script and put *me* on the defensive just to get an idea of what's at stake.

If you were to say that this whole book about metaphor theory and following Jesus is *rot*, that the author is an idiot, that you've never read anything so ridiculous and heretical, and that you would rate it "zero stars, do not recommend," I would not only be *hurt*, I would be *angry*. I would most naturally understand and experience your negative comments as a personal attack and it would be both natural and culturally acceptable for me to defend

my book from your unfair and unjust criticism, perhaps even by launching a counterattack on the creep who fired the first shot.

Your unkind words may elicit a psychosomatic response in me appropriate to physical conflict. A surge of adrenaline means my pulse would quicken and my blood pressure would rise. My neck and ears might turn red. I would probably feel flushed and begin to breathe more heavily. I'd clench my fists and jut out my chin and perhaps even curl my lip. My *body* would get me ready for one of two options: fight or flight.

Without conscious effort, I will experience the person who made those unwarranted comments about my book as an opponent, adversary, or even enemy. If you and I got into a debate over the quality or content of my writing, I would therefore seek to exploit any weakness in your argument as I try to shore up my own position. The objective in our verbal sparring would not be mutual benefit or understanding; instead, the most common goals for armed conflict—complete annihilation or absolute capitulation—will tend to be my goals for the outcome of that conversation. And you'll fight back with a similar aim.

So watch it! Don't go criticizing my book! Because for me and the people in my culture, Argument is War! We don't have to think about it. We don't take time to reflect on our options. If we feel under attack, we fight back.

Like all the lenses we have explored, the conceptual metaphor Argument is War does more than shape the way we *talk about* verbal disagreements. **The expectations and logic, the emotions and evaluations that apply to the situation of physical conflict shape the experience, expectations, emotions, and actions in the situation of verbal disagreement, as well.**

As Lakoff and Johnson put it: "Many of the things we *do* in arguing are partially structured by the concept of war... It is in this sense that the ARGUMENT IS WAR metaphor is one that we live by in this culture; it structures the actions we perform in arguing."[1]

---

[1] I've cited this important work a few times already: George Lakoff and Mark Johnson, *Metaphors We Live By* (get the 2003 reprint edition), page 4. Notice how in 2003 they were still using ALL CAPS to signify a conceptual metaphor. Today it would probably be more common to write "Argument is War."

This warfare mentality is all around us. Just think of how you see disagreements portrayed in sports or politics or social media or the news. Our culture can't talk about the color of a dress (gold or black?) or promote a candidate (red or blue?) without falling into the trap of reductionist, either/or posturing: **you are either *for us* or *against us*.**[2]

And since the *right* answer is so natural and obvious, it's also natural to assume that if you disagree with us you must be either *stupid* or *evil*. If you don't see what is self-evidently right, you must be *stupid*; if you *do* see what's obvious and natural but still fight against it, you must be *evil*. (Not that we mean to feel that way, but come on! How can they *not* see the obvious truth??)

The Church under Siege

Breathing the air in that kind of Argument is Warfare culture affects how you experience your faith and how you interact with people who don't think like you or act like you or believe like you. You don't have to go out of your way to feel embattled; you will naturally and automatically default to *fight or flight* when a perceived enemy does or says something you translate as an attack.

You don't *have* to do it that way.

You don't *choose* to do it that way.

You're not to *blame* for doing it that way.

When Outsiders start poking at things you hold dear, our culture tells you to circle the wagons or launch a counteroffensive. *Attacking* someone who doesn't think like you or act like you or believe like you counts as *defending* the Truth. And *defending* something you value sure feels good!

We're back to Container thinking again (see Chapter 6: Bank Vault or Banquet?). The strong dichotomy between Us and Them flows from the In vs Out logic of Containers. Recall that the key factor of the Container concept is the Boundary that serves to distinguish *and protect* what's on the Inside from what's on the Outside. And the stronger the Boundary, the *safer* the contents.

---

[2] One of my favorite descriptions of *you are either or us or against us* is "This Video Will Make You Angry" (https://youtu.be/rE3j_RHkqJc) from CGP Grey.

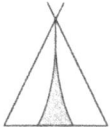

In a literal land war, we conceive of nations or other geographical regions as Containers whose Boundaries are established by their borders. It's natural, then, for a nation to protect its borders and count any violation of that invisible line as an act of war. The stronger your border defenses, the safer your country.

Container and Boundary thinking play important roles in *any* area of life we structure in terms of conflict. In sports, for example, you *defend* your goal or your side of the field, and *attack* your opponents. You know whose side you are on by the boundary lines or goal lines, as well as identity markers (like uniforms) that distinguish *us* from *them*.

I played *defense* on my soccer team in college, and while I occasionally strayed across the midline, my primary job was to mark the opposing team's offensive players when they came onto our side of the field. If they got anywhere near our eighteen yard box, the sense of danger got dialed up. (The more valuable the thing you are protecting, the higher the emotional stakes.) If they crossed into my territory to defend, my job was to take them out by any means necessary, even if it meant an intentional foul. Get too close to my goal, and I became a very *offensive* defenseman. It was pitched battle on the soccer pitch!

The emotions, logic, hoped-for outcomes, reasonable actions, and physical responses appropriate to pitched battle make up the situational *lens* or *frame* or *situational logic* we use to live out verbal disagreement in our culture. Whenever we feel like our Boundary is being violated, one natural instinct will be to attack.

In the Church, the same Boundary issues we saw in the last chapter—moral, social, political, and doctrinal—define the places where Outsiders will bump into our identity markers and encounter our strongest defenses.

Of course, you know you are supposed to welcome visitors to your congregation. But as soon as that visitor does or says something that crosses the line, they will quickly move from *guest* to *threat*. If you happen to be out in the world, where no such burden of hospitality exists, then you will be even more likely to respond to perceived attacks with emotions and logic and actions appropriate to defense (or counterattack).

For those on the Inside, those church Boundary issues will feel natural and obvious and self-evidently *true* (even if the specifics change by region or over

time[3]). Outsiders who don't see the world the way we do will therefore appear either willfully wrong (stupid) or intentionally set against God's Truth (evil).

If the "right" moral, political, and theological answers are natural and obvious, then *those people out there* who don't act or believe like we do are a threat to our faith. It's us against them, and there can be only one winner and one loser. We might be able to "live and let live," except that, as soon as their way of living crosses our boundary lines, that's an act of war. We have no choice but to engage in battle or face annihilation.

I'm not judging the Church.

I'm not accusing you of anything.

I'm just noticing: Hey, guys! This looks like our default setting! I wonder if that matters...?

Maybe you remember the indignation that arose when Starbuck's came out with a new, red coffee cup for the holiday season, one that didn't say "Merry Christmas" on it. (I can't believe it's been almost 10 years...) It doesn't matter that Starbuck's never pretended to be a Christian institution. It doesn't matter that the job of a secular business is not to tell people about Jesus. It doesn't even matter that Starbuck's *never had "Merry Christmas" printed on any of their cups in the first place*: as soon as people heard that the coffee house had *removed* that Christian greeting, it *felt* like an attack. And once you have framed your venti dark roast with no room as a battlefield of the culture wars, you respond with the emotions, attitudes, logic, and actions appropriate to Argument is War. Which is to say, some good Christian people said and did some things online that align with warfare and armed conflict more than with following Jesus.[4]

But can you blame them?

---

[3] I read recently that *forks* were considered *unchristian* in Medieval Europe. Eating your food with a fork was a clear and obvious rejection of *the hands* God gave us to do the job. Rejecting God's gifts is the same as rejecting God, so only pagans and heretics would consider using forks to eat their food. That seemingly humorous anecdote is a serious reminder of how what seems true and obvious can turn out to be less than universal or divinely ordained.

[4] I was reminded of the red Starbuck's cup by reading the introduction to Ed Stetzer, *Christians in the Age of Outrage: How to Bring Our Best When the World is at its Worst* (Tyndale Momentum, 2018). I didn't realize that Starbuck's couldn't have *removed* Merry Christmas from their cups, since they never had cups that said Merry Christmas in the first place!

Once you perceive a statement or action *as an attack* (even if the action didn't exist), you automatically go into Warfare mode. You draw up the battle lines and defend the boundary between *us* and *them*.

In a war, different rules apply. In a fight for survival, there are no small issues. When a pitched battle rages all around you, you don't have time for things like curiosity or empathy; and fraternizing with the enemy is an act of treason.

If what is being attacked is important or precious to you, you will be that much more likely to respond with force. (You can make fun of *me*, but don't mess with my kids!) So if you are emotionally invested in your life of faith, and I hope that you are, then when someone is perceived as crossing the line, or attacking your community, or your church history, or your Bible, or *your Jesus*, then your response will likely be emotionally charged, swift, and powerful.

Kill or be killed! Down with Starbuck's! Our Christian way of life is at stake!

The point is not to disparage the people who got caught up in the red cup non-controversy. The people who reacted with such outrage were simply living out a response that seemed reasonable at the time, at least from within our culture's dominant way of dealing with conflict. As soon as they saw the blank red cup as an *attack* on something they held dear, the Argument is War mentality kicked in: blow the other side out of the water.

Once the battle lines have been drawn, you don't really have a choice. If you don't jump in with your own comment or share the boycott on your Facebook page, you must not really love Jesus or Christmas. **The vehemence of your response becomes a litmus of your devotion; not taking a side isn't a viable option in War.**

Instead of rolling your eyes (or shaking your fist) at such an obvious over-reaction, recognize that, as long as you live in a culture dominated by Argument is War, you are only one red cup away from behaving just as badly.

You only need to interpret one word, one gesture, one facial expression or action as an *attack* and your body, mind, and emotions will all suggest possible responses appropriate to armed conflict. You don't have time to think about it; you don't *need* time to think about it. You *just know* how to respond. (And, of course, the best defense is a good offense...)

Who is My Enemy?

So how does the Bible invite us to think about and experience conflict? The answer is complicated. The biblical authors, writing at different moments in world history during the rise and fall of empires, often experience *literal* warfare with *literal* enemies and *actual* armed conflict. The Bible also uses the imagery of warfare to filter our experience of conflict or struggle or challenge in areas that are not actual battles at all. Sometimes, it's even hard to tell the difference.[5]

At a time when armed conflict and theological conflict overlapped and enemy *nations* also worshipped enemy *gods*, you might expect an *us vs them*, *take no prisoners* kind of mindset. If you let foreigners and their foreign gods stay in the land, they will eventually lead you into idolatry and pagan practices (which is indeed what happened).

But Moses not only gave commands that make the irreducibility of the conflict clear, he also included things like "love the foreigner in your midst, because you were foreigners in Egypt" (Deuteronomy 10:19). The Law prohibited marrying enemies for good reason (from Ahab in the North to Solomon in the South, we see a tragic pattern play out: foreign wives = foreign gods = apostasy and idolatry). Still, we see key exceptions where outsiders are grafted into the people of God (like the foreigners Rahab and Ruth, both in the ancestral line of David and Jesus).

The Psalms and Prophets know all about an experience of enemies. The Psalms can not only pray for rescue and protection from our enemies, they can pray for defeat or even destruction of our enemies. The prophets ironically point out that you should be careful what you pray for: if you want all of God's enemies to be annihilated, you should probably be aware of how your sin has made *you* one of those enemies you are asking God to wipe out!

By the time we get to the New Testament, the enemy armies are Roman rather than Egyptian, Assyrian, Babylonian, or Persian. The country Jesus knew growing up was divided in the middle by a region of hated, enemy

---

[5] See the prophet Joel, for example. Is he talking about enemy armies in terms of a horde of locusts? Or is he seeing an invading swarm of locusts as if they were enemy soldiers, armed for battle? As soon as you think you know, the text seems to say the opposite...

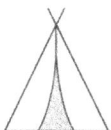

Samaritans and occupied throughout by hated, enemy Roman soldiers. But in the Sermon on the Mount (Matthew 5-7), Jesus teaches things like "turn the other cheek" or "if someone forces you to walk one mile with them, walk two" (a possible reference to Roman soldiers forcing people to carry their packs). When asked, "Who is my neighbor?" (Luke 10) Jesus responds with a story about a "good" Samaritan, an oxymoron for most of his audience: Samaritans are the bad guys by definition.

Jesus preaches an end to violence, hostility, and enmity. And yet, the same Jesus whose birth was heralded by angels as bringing peace on earth (Luke 2) can also say, "I have come not to bring peace, but a sword" (Matthew 10). The same Jesus who sends the disciples out to the "lost sheep of the house of Israel" (still Matthew 10) also sends the same disciples out "as sheep among wolves" (wait for it ... Matthew 10).

So which is it? Are those outside the faith *sheep* in need of guidance and protection and provision? Or are they *wolves,* who pose a dangerous and often deadly threat? **Within the collage of the disciples' experience, these seemingly contradictory perspectives or snapshots can both be true.** *Both* provide a helpful lens for interpreting (and therefore thinking, feeling, and acting in) *different* kinds of situations. The collage needs both perspectives. And it takes Wisdom to discern *which* snapshot is relevant to the present circumstance.[6]

We find a similar kind of complexity in the rest of the New Testament. In one place, Paul can call down anathemas on anyone who preaches a different Gospel (Galatians 1), yet in a different place say that, because of our fundamental unity in Jesus, *hostility itself* has been *put to death* (Ephesians 2). Paul can say that our real enemies are not physical, but spiritual (and therefore we need the "armor of God" Ephesians 6); but can also say with tears, that "many live as enemies of the cross of Christ" and admit that we are in desperate need of being rescued by a Savior from the country of our heavenly citizenship (Philippians 3).

---

[6] If you skipped Chapter 5 (What You See is What You Get), you might want to go back and check it out. It discusses the relationship between snapshots and a collage as well as the situational nature of metaphor and the role Wisdom plays in discerning between different ways of framing your experience.

Paul seems to think that there are times when believers will experience *even other people* as enemies or captors. In that situation, *longing for rescue* is a faithful response. But Paul also seems to think that the real battle supersedes any disagreements with mere humans. In that case, preparing for *spiritual warfare* is a reasonable reaction.

So how does the Bible invite us to experience conflict? The answer is complicated. The above examples are only a few of the vast number of snapshots the Scriptures give us for interpreting different situations of struggle, tension, or conflict. But even in this brief survey, we can begin to see the variety and complexity of the collage.

That complexity is worth fighting for. **One natural responses to conflict is to ignore complexity and over-simplify.** If a circumstance counts as armed conflict, there is no room for nuance and no for need options: if you are being shot at, you either run and hide or shoot back.

But Wisdom invites us to consider which lenses are appropriate for which situations. If you only have one snapshot, you cannot be faithful to the collage. If all you have is launch codes, everything looks like thermonuclear war. And mutually assured destruction somehow feels like a reasonable outcome...

Argument is Dance

War isn't just one possible way we *could* choose to experience Argument in our culture. War is *the default setting* for how we perceive, imagine, and live out all kinds of disagreements in every sector of our society. **As long as Warfare thinking is *the only way* we navigate the challenges of interacting with people who don't agree with us (inside the Church) or don't believe like us (outside the Church), our default choices will boil down to defense, attack, or counterattack.** (Or maybe retreat, if things seem to be going poorly...)

The way to get around that dangerous cultural default is to have more options available to you, to try on different lenses, to keep other ways of framing the same situation in your bag. Even if your knee-jerk reaction conforms to the

shape of armed conflict, having other lenses available will make other kinds of options seem plausible (or even possible).

In the section of *Metaphors We Live By* that identifies Argument is War, authors Lakoff and Johnson suggest "Argument is Dance" as a possible alternative. They really just mention the possibility in passing to show that War isn't the *only* option. But taking time to explore Dance as a possible lens for Argument makes the logic inherent in the situation clear.[7]

To start, consider how the Warfare lens shapes your own understanding of an Argument. Say someone makes a critical or disparaging remark that you take as an "attack" on something you value or know to be true. You will automatically go into defense mode (like I did when you said those nasty things about my book). The battle lines are drawn. As you engage in that argument, you will naturally seek to exploit the weaknesses of your opponent (as you attack) and automatically try to shore up your own position (as you defend).

To avoid escalating the situation, you might limit your response to something appropriate. At the same time, you'll want to make sure you give as well as you get. If I stomp on your toes in a barroom brawl, you might reasonably be expected to kick me in the shins. That response would be measured and reasonable and even appropriate given the scale of violence involved. If I attack your opinion about the color of the church carpet and you start talking trash about my mother, that could be seen as "fighting dirty." The counterattack far outweighs the original violence. So keep it clean.

Your primary goal in this struggle will *not* be collaboration or mutual benefit or even understanding the other side. You don't need to *understand* the enemy unless it helps you neutralize them. The hoped-for outcomes in armed conflict apply here, so complete annihilation or absolute capitulation will tend to be your goals for the outcome of that conversation.

You aren't trying to make the Truth attractive or winsome or reasonable; those idiots who don't believe like you do have already shown they are completely unreasonable, if not downright evil. So you will judge your success

---

[7] See Chapter 5, above, especially the section "Situational Thinking and Discipleship."

or failure in terms of how much damage you took compared to how much damage you inflicted. (I may have black eye, but you should see the other guy!)

That's how the Warfare frame guides and enables the activity of Argument. Now, take off the glasses called *Warfare* for a moment, and put on the lenses of *Dance*. When you do, the exact same situation has a different kind of logic. Other emotions, evaluations, expectations, and outcomes come into focus.

Wearing Dance lenses, that opening salvo becomes in invitation to collaboration and engagement, not a perceived attack. The appropriate response to "Let's dance!" is excitement, interest, curiosity, and expectation (not hurt, anger, defensiveness, or aggression). That shot of adrenaline gets your body ready to *move*, not just to *fight*.

If Argument is a kind of Dance, any weakness or deficiency in your dialogue partner's argument is no longer a chink in the armor you are supposed to exploit. Instead, any misstep, injury, or lack of skill or knowledge for either partner becomes an obstacle that can get in the way of an enjoyable dance for both; so both will work together to make up for any mistake.

In a Dance, you don't guard your territory or defend your borders. You naturally move back as your partner moves forward; then you move forward as your partner moves back. This give and take is a natural, essential part of the Dance that allows fluid movement. Defending your turf would be self-defeating.

If I stomp on your toes in a brawl, you kick me in the shins. If I step on your toes during a dance, however, kicking me in the shins would not even come into question as an available response because the situational logic of dance doesn't have "counterattack" as a viable option. You would do your best to cover up my mistake so we could get back to the joy of the dance.

Your aim would no longer be to "win" the argument. (You can't "win" a dance.) Instead, the hoped-for outcome of our verbal interaction would be mutual enjoyment and benefit, for us and any observers, and maybe even a stronger relationship between us. Success would be measured in terms of participation: dancing *together* is both the activity and the goal.

Along the way, you wouldn't view your dance partner as a threat or an enemy (or an idiot). You *need* a partner for this dance to take place! The physical

tension and energy and movement back and forth is part of what enables dance and makes the experience fun. You aren't just hoping to get through the experience unscathed; you are enjoying yourself along the way.

Unfortunately, we don't have Argument is Dance as an alternative in our system of cultural defaults. But imagining (or even experimenting with) that different lens shows **we can come up with other options.** Structuring Argument in terms of Dance would change not only how we talk about disagreement, but how we experience, live out, and evaluate the act of disagreeing. When the metaphor changes, even the expectations and rules of engagement change!

Experimenting with Dance as a frame for Argument in my own personal interactions leads me to think that it may actually be a viable and vibrant substitute for Argument is War. Can we can come up with any other filters or ways of framing the situation of disagreement that could give us more options for evaluating, feeling, and acting in the real world?

The Tension Trellis

Back in Chapter 5, we followed Jesus and the disciples into the foreign territory of Samaria. We saw how the disciples evaluated that situation through a lens of *defiling enemy outsiders.* Jesus says to them: "Look, lift up your eyes, and see." Jesus then invites his followers to view their current circumstances through a different lens, one he calls "the fields ripe for harvest."[8]

That story in John 4 isn't devoid of disagreement or verbal tension. You could interpret the tête-à-tête between Jesus and the Samaritan woman at the well as head-to-head theological melee. But Jesus seems to experience this back and forth more like a dance. By the end of the scene, Jesus is asking his disciples (who must feel like they are surrounded by enemies) to see the oncoming crowd of Samaritan villagers through a horticultural lens, not a hostile one.

Notice: Jesus doesn't shy away from tension or disagreement. He just doesn't process that tension through the lens of Warfare. He knows that people

---

[8] See Chapter 5, above, especially the section "The Invitation to Change Your Lens."

like the Samaritan woman (and the rest of her village) won't read the Bible the same way he does or believe what he believes about worship or food laws or even the Messiah. But his words and actions and demeanor are not *defensive*. His posture is not a kind of *attack*.

Instead, we find Jesus asking for hospitality and inviting people into dialogue, so much so that he will end up staying three days in this foreign village. The disciples are left with the choice of either *receiving Samaritan hospitality* (something I'm sure they hated to do) or *abandoning Jesus* (something they were committed *not* to do). In the end, the disciples stay, and the whole village of outsiders comes to know and believe in Jesus as *their* Messiah, too.

Jesus didn't score points against the opposing team. Jesus didn't defend his position. Jesus didn't blow anyone out of the water.

Jesus also didn't ignore the tension; instead, he used the tension as an excuse for invitation and a platform for growth.

If you've ever played in a band or orchestra, if you've ever gotten past the first few piano lessons, then you know that *dissonance* is an important element of music. The tension between those notes that seem to clash so violently provides movement toward resolution. Dissonance isn't the same as playing out of tune; dissonance is two or more notes sounding at the same time in a kind of tension that provides traction to move the music forward.

If you've ever planted peas or string beans, you know that a simple string under tension can provide a trellis those vines need to grow and flourish. In fact, much like an orchestra, an entire garden is working together not merely on the basis of their similarities, but by adding to the whole by virtue of their differences. One plant needs more sun; one needs shade. One puts nutrients back into the soil that another needs to thrive.

Tension, in a dance or orchestra or garden, provides a necessary force for movement and growth.[9] Dissonance and difference are not the same as conflict. Medley is not a form of melee. The peas don't wish they could avoid

---

[9] Sam Wells talks about tension in a congregation in terms of symphony and horticulture in his book *A Nazareth Manifesto: Being with God* (Kindle Edition, 56-59). Friendly caution: do NOT judge that book by its cover!

the trellis altogether. The trombones don't win when the violins lose. (Though some trombone players might think otherwise.)

Even *resolution* doesn't mean returning to a state before the tension took place. Dissonance and difference are important dynamics that move the music forward, toward something new. They help the garden change as well as grow.[10]

That's what I see in Jesus in John 4, with his disciples, the woman at the well, and the crowd of Samaritans who eventually invite him to stay a few days. I don't suspect Jesus ever played in an orchestra or grew string beans (though he does use a harvest metaphor in John 4). I do think his engagement with the woman, the disciples, and the crowd shows an attitude toward dissonance and tension and that embodies music and gardening rather than attack and defense.

What would happen if we took those same attitudes into our conversations, our cultural controversies, and our interpersonal conflicts? **What if we saw *tension* as a necessary building block for deeper relationships, *difference* as a prerequisite for growth, and *dissonance* as a spark of creative energy that leads to new possibilities?**

Could we change the default setting on that jolt of adrenaline that comes when we recognize a moment of disagreement? Could that chemical reaction in the brain ever automatically indicate curiosity and engagement—the first steps in a dance—instead of our conditioned response of fight or flight?

Honestly, maybe not.

Argument is War is so ingrained in our cultural experience that we may never be able to develop a knee-jerk reaction of curiosity to replace our default reaction of defense. But it's worth a try.

And, more importantly, **your first, knee-jerk reaction doesn't have to be your *only* reaction.** Even if your first inclination is fight or flight, you can practice taking a step back and re-evaluating your situation through the lens of dance, or music, or gardening before firing off your response. You can hold onto openness and curiosity and respect even when your first impulse is a closed fist.

---

[10] "Reconciliation is not the restoration of an untroubled condition before a conflict; it is the creation of something that might never have been without that conflict." Sam Wells, *A Nazareth Manifesto* (Kindle Edition, 58).

You can hear Jesus say to you: "Look, lift up your eyes, and see." Maybe Harvest is a more fruitful metaphor than Warfare in this situation.

It may take Wisdom to discern which lens best fits your current circumstances, but you do have options. Warfare isn't the only way to frame disagreement. Winning isn't the only valuable goal in dialogue. Attack and defense aren't the only tools you have in your bag.

The Hospitality Tent

As we saw in Chapter 6, containers function to keep separate things separate and to protect what's on the inside from what's on the outside. In a similar way, Warfare thinking divides the world into Us and Them; and collusion with the enemy is not only frowned upon, it is a capital offense.

While Warfare and Container thinking keeps us separate from people who aren't like us, Hospitality invites us into closer contact with both friends and strangers. *Offering* hospitality means inviting outsiders across borders and boundary lines to join you on the inside. *Receiving* hospitality means entering someone else's home territory and accepting it as your own. As we also saw in Chapter 6, the mission and ministry of Jesus is often lived out in terms of offering or receiving hospitality.

Hospitality isn't the *only* snapshot Jesus uses to frame his purpose; a kind of Warfare is also a part of the collage. But in contrast to our cultural conditioning, Hospitality seems to be the default setting for Jesus. Apart from special circumstances or a specific kind of context, the knee-jerk reaction we see in Jesus when he interacts with people who don't think or believe like he does has to do with inviting them in or going over to their place for dinner. It's almost as if Jesus intentionally wants to spend time in the presence of people who don't (yet) see the world the way he does.

You might even say that spending time with people is the whole point of the incarnation. Of course, Jesus came to save. He came to die and rise again, to take away the sins of the world and to defeat sin, death, and the devil.

But in a fundamental sense, all of those saving actions of Jesus flow from God's desire to be *with us*. From the very beginning, God walked with us in the Garden (Genesis 2). When sin entered the world, God promised to put warfare between the Offspring of Eve and the serpent (Genesis 3), so that God could be with us again. After the nations are scattered in the aftermath of the Tower of Babel (Genesis 11), God chooses one nation in order to bless all the nations of the earth (Genesis 12). When that nation of Israel heads out of Egypt and into the wilderness, God knows they are still a sinful people. In some sense, they are still enemies. But God wants to go with them, anyway.

So God commands Moses to build a dwelling place, a tent—*The Tent*, in fact—the Tent of Meeting, or Tabernacle, where the very presence of Yahweh comes down to dwell in the midst of a rebellious people.

When we catch a glimpse of the End of the whole Story, the final victory is also framed in terms of *being with*. John sees the New Jerusalem coming down out of heaven from God and hears a great voice say,

> "Look! The dwelling place (or tabernacle, or tent) of God is now among the people, and God will dwell (or tabernacle, or tent) *with them*, and they will be God's Own People, and the Very God will be their God."
>
> Revelation 21:3

God dwelling with us was the original design. *God dwelling with us* is what Jesus came to restore. *God with us* is the job description Jesus fulfills in his mission and ministry. *God with us* is the motivation, goal, and substance of who Jesus is and what Jesus does.[11]

So when John describes the incarnation of the eternal Logos of God in his opening chapter, he uses vocabulary that belongs to the Garden of Eden, the Tent of Meeting, and the New Jerusalem all at once:

> The Word became flesh and *made his dwelling* among us.
>
> John 1:14 (NIV)

---

[11] The central argument of Sam Wells, *A Nazareth Manifesto*, is the priority of *being with* over other modes of interaction like doing with or doing for.

Jesus *tented* with us.

Jesus *tabernacled* with us.

Yes, Jesus came to die and rise. But first, he came to *just be with us*.

And the point of his dying and rising was to open the way for us to be with him, forever.

A tent isn't a fortress. You can't defend it very well. But that vulnerability also makes it portable. You can take a tent with you to provide a home away from home anyplace you go.

That's kind of what the Tabernacle was during the forty years of wandering: a home away from home, a portable Garden of Eden even in the arid wilderness.

That's kind of what Jesus was during his earthly ministry: the place where heaven meets earth, where God can tent among the people, where sins are forgiven and enemies welcomed home.

Tenting among the people so they can have access to God: that's what Jesus lived out in Nazareth and Galilee and Jerusalem, but also across the border in a Samaritan village and in foreign territory with a Syrophoenician woman.

Tenting among the people so they can have access to God: that's a good description of the mission and ministry of the Church. If, as Paul says, we are being built together into a dwelling place where God lives by the power of the Spirit (Ephesians 2), then we together as Church are a portable Temple, the place where heaven meets earth, where God can tent among the people once more and sins are forgiven and enemies welcomed home.

That's such a different vision for what it means to be Church! If *culture wars* define your experience and *attack and defense* are the way you encounter the world around you, then you will want to keep the boundaries between Us and Them as strong and impenetrable as possible. If, on the other hand, you want to live out your calling as a kind of tent or Tabernacle or dwelling place of the Most High God, then you will prioritize *being with* people over defending yourself or your theology from them.

But that is so hard! A tent, by definition, is a dwelling whose portable walls are held up by tension. But when we experience tension, our automatic

reaction is to draw battle lines and either retreat or attack. Simply *being with* is not a good tactic when it comes to war.

As soon as the opinions or actions of others violate the boundary issues of your local faith community, you will feel like your church and your faith are under attack. If they don't believe that Jesus is God, or that God created the world, or that the Bible is reliable, you will naturally want to defend the truth of your theology. If they don't vote like you or have the same moral compass as you or don't value the things you value, you will see a clear opening for a counterattack. If Starbuck's "removes" *Merry Christmas* from their holiday coffee cups, it may well feel like an act of war.

So how do you flip the switch from *attack* mode to *tent* mode when faced with someone who doesn't think, believe, or live like you do? How do you manage *being with* when just being with someone pushes your buttons?

Tent Thinking in a World of Enemies

Earlier this year, I got to hear a friend present at a church workers conference. His talk was about *not* viewing outsiders as enemies. In the Q&A afterward, a version of that question about changing your default came up.

Actually, several important questions came up and, talking to my friend later, I learned that these kinds of questions usually get raised whenever he gives a presentation on the Church not treating the world as an enemy.

The first objection was a kind of *yeah, but...* "Yeah, but what if they *really are* my enemy? What if they come into the church with a gun and start shooting people? What if they want to destroy Christianity? You say not to treat outsiders like enemies, but *what if they really are??*"

My friend began his answer with something like the snapshot and collage discussion we have pursued in this book: there may be a time and place when the filter of Enemy or Warfare actually does apply. But not nearly as often or as permanently as we tend to assume...

Then he went on to talk about the importance of putting that experience of enemies into a broader story. **When I experience someone as *an enemy*, I am experiencing them through the lens of *my own story*.** They are getting in the

way of my goals and objectives. They are a threat to my agenda or my well-being. In the story of My Life, where I am the hero, I will experience people opposed to me as villains. And in that moment, in *my* story, the guy who comes into my church with a gun *is clearly the enemy.*

That analysis happens automatically at the level of my story. And it's not wrong. You probably *should* treat the guy with a gun like an enemy for the purposes of your worship service.

But that's not the *only* story that encompasses that experience. **If I view that same situation through the lens of Jesus and his story, then things look different.** All of a sudden I see that man with a gun as someone with a history and a future. I see a sinner for whom Christ died. I see a man in the middle of an act that will do damage to himself and his friends and family, an act that is nonetheless not outside grace or forgiveness.

I realize I don't know how the shooter's story will end, because Jesus isn't done with his story yet. I am struck by the fact that, from the perspective of Jesus and his story, I am just as much in need of repentance and forgiveness and redemption as this guy.

He may tragically be shooting at me and my family in this moment, and in this moment he is unequivocally my enemy. **But this moment is not the defining moment for him or for me, because Jesus is still at work—*in him* and *in me.*** In terms of my story, he is momentarily my enemy. In terms of Jesus' story, that man is my fellow sinner and fellow redeemed; a brother for whom Christ died; someone I may possibly (Lord, have mercy) greet with joy in the resurrection of the dead and life of the world to come.

So what if that stranger or outsider *really is* my enemy? I will hold *my story* in tension with the knowledge that *the story of Jesus* is bigger than my experience. The guy with a gun may really be an enemy in my story. But my story isn't the story that matters most, even to me.

That guy with the gun scenario is just one typical discussion that comes from talking about not treating the culture around us as The Enemy. Another question that gets raised regularly is some version of, "So how do you flip the switch from *Pitched Battle* to *Pitched Tent* when you encounter someone who

doesn't think, believe, or live like you do?" (Of course, they wouldn't use the language of battles and tents, but you get the idea.)

My friend responds to that kind of question by saying: *slow down*. Here's what I think he means by that.[12] When you are caught up in *Pitched Battle* mode, you feel a lot of pressure and maybe some panic. It's important to get this settled quickly, to get the enemy to capitulate, to defend your ground before you lose it.

When you engage in conversation with someone on the other side of moral, political, or theological boundary lines, the stakes feel high and the time table feels short. If you don't correct their view in the next five minutes, they may never get their opinion changed! And because having the *right* opinion about immigration or taxes or private school funding is important to you, and knowing the *truth* about the divinity of Jesus or the inspiration of Scripture is *really* important to you—and you know how important all that is for *them*, too (even if they don't)—you experience the whole encounter with **a real sense of urgency.**

Your identity feels under attack, and you must respond immediately. Their eternal salvation is at stake, and you may not get a second chance to convince them of their errors. The whole encounter is fraught with the burden of having to articulate and defend a clear expression of the Truth, the whole Truth, and nothing but the Truth *as quickly as possible*. Every social, moral, and theological boundary line is connected to all others, so you must be ready to defend every area of church history and theology and every political or moral issue whenever anyone bumps into any contested territory. And do it quickly.

In a battle, the stakes and the urgency are high. An army spends a lot of time sitting around waiting. But when the warfare starts, there is no time to lose!

That's why my friend's advice is: *slow down*. When you slow down, you have time for curiosity and clarifying questions. You can wonder about the person in front of you and what brought them to that position or opinion. You

---

[12] The presentation this Q&A session followed was based on the book *Christ, Church, and World: Bonhoeffer and Lutheran Ecclesiology after Christendom* by Theodore J. Hopkins (Fortress Academic, 2021), especially Chapter 4. Ted is the friend I was telling you about.

can dial down the pressure on yourself and on the conversation. You can listen for what they are actually saying instead of preparing your next artillery shell. You don't have to convince them of *anything* in the next five minutes.

That kind of attitude is like pitching a tent and inviting someone in. We're going to be here for a while, can I get you something to drink?

In pitched battle, your *strength* and *ability to withstand the other* are vitally important. When you pitch a tent in the midst of a wandering people, your *humility* and *ability to understand the other* become key.

When the whole point of the conversation is *being with* the other person, rather than convincing them, or rebuffing them, or converting them, then you have time. You can slow down and even enjoy yourself.

It's not easy. But when I have managed, at least for a little while, to flip the switch from Pitched Battle to Pitched Tent, I have found curiosity and delight to be key elements of the conversation.

If tension or difference are important for movement and growth, then I can wonder what I might learn from this person or from our interaction. I can be open to the gift Jesus is giving me through this other person. I can ask questions and seek to understand. I can engage my ears as well as my imagination. I can actively look for something in the other person I respect or admire. I can affirm and engage their unique story and perspective without having to agree with every one of their ideas.

I can slow down and enjoy myself. I can slow down and enjoy *them*.

So the next time someone steps on your toes in a conversation, think of it as a dance. Interpret that shot of adrenaline as an invitation to curiosity. Notice the dissonance or tension, and get a little excited about the possibility of movement or growth.

The next time someone seems to attack what you believe, take a deep breath and wonder: What can I learn from them? What gift is Jesus giving me through them? How can I affirm something in them? What delights me about them?

Don't try to score points. (If I feel like I landed *a really good zinger*, I know I am no longer dancing.) Instead, try to enjoy *being with* the person in front of you.

And if you have people in your life who *really are* your enemies, then go ahead and treat them that way; that is to say, cry out to God for rescue from your enemies, and then "love your enemies and pray for those who persecute you" (Mathew 10 yet again). Acknowledge the actions and attitudes that make them enemies in your story; then zoom out to the story of Jesus and try to see them (and yourself) differently.

If you are aware of the fact that your cultural default is to resort to Warfare whenever there's an Argument, then you are able to slow down your immediate response. Even if your knee-jerk reaction is to attack or defend, you can look for other available ways of framing the situation. You have options.

In a world that values pitched battle as the primary mode of interaction with strangers and outsiders, you can pitch your tent and invite people in.

You don't have to defend Jesus from all those people out there who don't know him or trust him or believe in him the same way you do.

You are part of the people who make up a portable dwelling place where God takes up residence by the power of the Spirit.

You are a mini-Tabernacle, a place where heaven meets earth, where Jesus is present for you; and present through you, for the world.

Jesus doesn't need protecting. But he will be with you as you experience enemies, learn from outsiders, and experiment with hospitality. In fact, *being with* you is the whole reason he came.

• • •

Summary of Chapter 7: Pitched Battle or Pitched Tent?

It seems like the most natural thing in the world to want to defend your faith, your Church, or even the Truth from enemies who attack from the outside. That knee-jerk reaction is reinforced by a standard default in our culture: we structure and experience Argument in terms of Warfare.

While the vast witness of Scripture does talk about having enemies, that experience is often more complicated or nuanced than we take time to notice, especially when we feel under attack.

Adding alternative frames for the experience of verbal disagreement gives us a chance to move on from our initial default reaction. We can begin to explore other possible kinds of responses. If we experience Argument in terms of Dance, Tension in terms of a Garden Trellis, or Disagreement as a form of Dissonance that moves the music forward, then our thinking, acting, and feeling will take a different form as we begin to look for a different outcome.

In Jesus, we see God's desire to be with us, even though we were his enemies. Jesus *tabernacles* in our midst, pitching his tent with us. That way of being in the world invites us to think less in terms of combat, with winners and losers, and more in terms of the Tent of Meeting, a portable dwelling where God's presence went with a sinful people as they wandered in the wilderness.

While we can and do still experience some people as enemies in some situations, the larger story of Jesus as *God with us* changes our default settings from Warfare to Hospitality, from Pitched Battle to Pitched Tent. Instead of feeling pressure to win every skirmish and defend every border issue, we are invited to enjoy being with the people God puts in front of us.

God's ultimate objective in creation, redemption, and new creation—to *be with* us—becomes our goal, as well. We want to spend time *being with*, getting to know, and learning from people who don't think or believe like we do.

Slow down. Stay curious. Look for options. And enjoy being with other people, even when you disagree with them. Jesus still has the ultimate victory and the ultimate corner on the Truth; and Jesus received hospitality from sinners so he could be with them.

Come, Holy Spirit, and shape Jesus in us!

This Changes Everything

 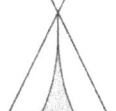

Pitched Battle   Pitched Tent

	Pitched Battle	Pitched Tent
Jesus	Jesus is the most valuable thing we have, so Jesus needs to be protected from those who attack us from the outside.	Jesus pitches his tent in the midst of a sinful world so he can *be with* us. Jesus is the place heaven meets earth. Jesus welcomes us in.
The Church	A castle with a moat. Wagons, circled. A fortress that defends the Gospel from the attacking world.	A portable dwelling place for God. A place to call home even while wandering in the wilderness.
The World	Enemies who attack Christians, the Church, and the truth of God's Word.	People Jesus loves to spend time *being with*; a field ripe for harvest; people to welcome in.
The Goal	Keep *Us* safe from *Them*. Attack vulnerable enemy positions. Either get the enemy to give in or blow them out of the water.	Spend time enjoying the people God has put in front of you. Receive the gift Jesus is giving you through the other person.
My Role	Defend the Gospel. Attack those who might attack the Gospel. Win every battle. Don't give an inch. Do NOT fraternize with the enemy, or you become the enemy.	Spend quality time *being with* Jesus. Spend quality time *being with* people who don't know Jesus. Slow down and enjoy people who aren't like me.
Key Thinking	Every battle has one winner and one loser. All's fair in war. Every theological position must be defended at all costs, every time it comes under attack. The best defense is a good offense. You are either *for us* or *against us*. Traitors are as bad as the enemy.	A tent is not very defensible, but it is portable and allows you to be with people on their journey. Just as Jesus delights in *being with* us, we delight in *being with* other people. The Truth is still true, but I invite people in and learn from them as we encounter the Truth together.

For Further Reflection

Think of an argument or disagreement you have had recently. In what ways did the dynamics of Warfare play out in that experience? Can you identify moments you felt defensive or started to attack the other person? Who "won"? How can you tell? What comes next?

When you feel under attack, do you tend towards fight or flight? Share an example. Why do you think you typically respond that way?

What people in your life do you experience as enemies? How do you process that experience with Jesus?

Which of the other options for responding to tension did you find most interesting: an invitation to dance, dissonance in an orchestra, or tension in a garden trellis? How could you experiment with those lenses?

What are the challenges of *being with* people in your life who don't think or believe or behave like you do? How might you take delight in people who are different from you? In what one way can you practice slowing down and just *being with* someone this week?

Conclusion

GPA or GPS?
Where do we go from here?

Trying on a New Hat

If you wear a stylish hat to work, or to a family gathering, or to a social event, you are making a statement. You are inviting people to evaluate you (or at least your fashion sense) based on that hat. But what if you are out shopping with some friends? Then trying on even the most eccentric headgear would no longer be a personal commitment. "Hey, guys—look at THIS! Whaddya think?"

At the beginning of any given semester at the London School of Theology, my friend Conrad would use that hat analogy to invite class participation. When you are discussing the specific words and context of a Pauline epistle as part of a New Testament course, you are not necessarily making a statement about your identity or giving your final answer on a theological position; you may well be trying on an idea to see if it fits, or even how outlandish it would be to wear. "Hey, guys—what about THIS?!"

In the midst of conversation, safely behind closed doors and surrounded by friends, you are allowed to "try on" different opinions, interpretations, or even theological implications without anyone judging your orthodoxy (or salvation).

That hat analogy reminds me of my very first semester at seminary. At the welcome meeting, the Dean of Students encouraged all of us newbies to fully engage our studies and not hold back our questions for fear of being wrong. "As

long as you are a student," he told us, "it's OK to be a heretic." The implication was, you are free to try on a new theological hat without worrying about how people will judge your fashion sense. Be wrong now, so you can be better later.

The fear of getting it wrong (and being a heretic) can get in the way of your theological education. But I think **the fear of getting it wrong gets in the way of following Jesus in every aspect of faith,** not just seminary training.

All the different lenses we have explored in this book are like different hats you have to try on to see how they look, what they would mean for your identity, who you might be if you wore this cowboy hat instead of that beret to the party. Sometimes you won't know until you actually wear it around for a while and try it with a few different outfits.

The fear of getting it wrong will lead you to wear the same old lenses you have always worn. And while *never changing* your comfortable old hat feels like it should protect you from heresy, wearing the exact same baseball cap to each and every social function makes its own kind of statement.

The context or situation determines what kind of fashion statement you are making. Put on a floppy cap in front of a mirror while shopping with friends and you are just trying it on. Wear it to class and it means something else. Wear it to your *wedding* and your fashion statement has shifted yet again. Different contexts may require different headgear; and the same hat will be interpreted differently in different contexts.

But that's just what we have been saying all along: the kinds of theological lenses you use to interpret a situation, to think, feel, and act faithfully, will shift *depending on the situation.* There is no one-size-fits-all interpretive fedora that fits every situation perfectly. (Recall the conversation about biblical Wisdom back in Chapter 5.)

If you are afraid of getting it wrong, you will be hesitant to change the metaphors you are living by in a particular setting. But the only sure way of getting the context wrong *most of the time* is to never change your hat at all. **Fear of heresy makes heretics of us all.**

Your Spiritual GPA and GPS

Fear of getting it wrong is often baked into our cultural psyche. As we saw back in Chapter 3, Good naturally seems to be Up for us. We assume we have to work harder and do better to achieve a higher standard and the rewards that come with being Up: more happiness, more money, more success, more *more*.

The obvious conclusion that Good is Up begins in our own bodily experience in the physical world and gets reinforced by the way people talk, reason, evaluate, and express their feelings in the culture around us.

One clear and pervasive example is the way we evaluate most students at most schools in our country. A grade point system evaluates you based on your performance and places you on a continuum with other students, a continuum structured in terms of Up and Down, where Good is Up.

Study hard, do better on your tests, get *higher* scores, and your GPA will go Up. Fail to study, fail to prepare well, fail to learn and you will fail that class (and your failure will be reflected in a *lower* Grade Point Average).

That GPA thinking doesn't die out after you graduate. Because you live in a performance-based culture, you will silently grade your financial status, your relational status, and even your spiritual status in terms of Up and Down, Good and Bad. You walk around with a subconscious GPA for your life that tells you how well you are doing compared to everyone else. (And probably that you should be working harder to do better.)

That default tendency can be so powerful in our culture, it will often seem natural and obvious to *grade your own performance* based on this book about what seems natural and obvious. I'm probably getting a C in Assembly Line over Adventure thinking, but our intergenerational youth group experiment deserves at least a B+. I flunked the Argument is Warfare exam, but I know people who did a lot worse. (Maybe we can grade that one on a curve?) Overall, I'm probably a low B or high C compared to some others I could mention, and with the help of this book, I'm sure I could work hard and do better...

You probably wouldn't say it out loud like that. But you might experience it that way. Every new insight, every new skill, every new way of seeing your faith play out in the real world naturally becomes an opportunity for you to do

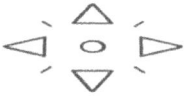

more or do better so you can be Good (and Up). Self-improvement is a bestselling category for a reason.

We all naturally imagine life in terms of a GPA, and we *just know* we could do a little better if we only had more or better information, or worked harder or smarter, or had the right cheat codes. And fear of getting it wrong is hardwired into a system based on maximizing success and avoiding failure.

So we need a different metaphor for living out the metaphors we live by in this book. We need an alternate way of thinking about, evaluating, and living out our defaults for thinking about, evaluating, and living out our faith. We need a way of experiencing the different ways of experiencing our relationship with Jesus, in community—a lens that helps us evaluate our lenses in a more helpful way. We need an alternate to our ingrained GPA mindset to guide the way we implement a new way of imagining faith and following.

Instead of a GPA default, we want to shift to a GPS approach to evaluating how we are doing with the personal and institutional changes suggested in this book. When we get away from a focus on performance, and instead focus on movement and direction, some wonderful things begin to happen.

Your Global Positioning System simply tells you *where you are*. Your GPS doesn't *judge you* based on where you are. It doesn't *grade you* based on where you are. Your GPS simply says, "You are here."

Add some movement and you get not only location but *direction*. Add a destination and you get *navigation*. Get really fancy and make your destination *a person* (I found out I can do this with my wife), and even if that person is moving, you can still navigate a path that gets you from where you are (no judgment) to where that other person is going to be.

"Where am I right now?" is a much better question than "How well am I doing?" It doesn't grade your performance; it shows you distance and direction. You don't get a lower grade for being farther away. And you can't evaluate your direction without some kind of movement. It kind of reminds me of the ultimate GPS statement in Scripture, when God says to Abraham in Genesis 12:1, "Go to the land I will show you." In other words, start moving and I'll let you know when we get there...

Shifting from a spiritual GPA to a spiritual GPS means you are no longer focusing on your performance; instead, you are checking your location and direction toward a destination. Because that destination is a person, your path may take some twists and turns, especially if that person is on the move or says something like, "Follow me."

When you fall down or get stuck or experience sin or failure, your GPA will tell you to *do more and try harder*. Your GPS says, this is where you are and where you are headed; and *this* is the direction you want to go instead.

You might feel like an idiot for taking a wrong turn. But your GPS doesn't care; here are four alternate routes that come with a similar ETA. Just keep moving forward and we will get there eventually.

So when it comes to implementing a Pitched Tent mentality instead of a Pitched Battle with the culture around you, when it comes to inviting people to a movable Banquet instead of locking your theology in a Bank Vault, when it comes to shifting from a Relay Race to a Rope Team or escaping the Assembly Line to join the Adventure, you will naturally evaluate yourself and your congregation in terms of your performance. You will want to do more and do better to get a better grade and a higher average. But that kind of performance-driven evaluation can kill even the best good news.

Instead, use the Rope Team or the Banquet or the Pitched Tent or the Adventure as a kind of compass. Check in regularly to notice where you are and where you are headed. Wonder what Jesus is up to next and commit to a path you know may need to change (since Jesus is still on the move).

Drop your own judgment of your own performance. Start evaluating movement and direction instead. Stop grading your faith life. Keep taking small steps forward. Don't get help from other people so you can work harder and do better; instead, get help from other people because we need others to help us see more clearly where we are and where Jesus is headed next.

Don't use this book as a GPA; do use it as a GPS.

And don't go it alone.

We Follow Jesus Better when We Follow Him Together

If you are a fish, it's not easy to discover water. Trying to think about *how we think* or reimagine *the way we imagine* faith and following can be a real challenge. What seems obvious and natural will rarely get a second thought. And those default settings are designed to be taken for granted. The harder our defaults are to see, the more stable a community you can build around them.[1]

So, like all areas of discipleship, learning to see (and change) what we all take for granted is a team sport. We need each other if we want to notice the defaults that determine so much of what we think, feel, and do in this life of faith.

If you are reading this book as an individual, I hope the way of approaching discipleship in these pages motivates you to share it with others. If you are reading this as a lay leader, I hope you will want to share it with other leaders. If you are a church professional, I hope you will want to engage your leadership team and congregation with the joy and challenge of following Jesus in more biblical (and more beautiful) ways.

As you think about sharing the tools and perspectives that have been most important to you in this book, I'd like to share a word of caution from a friend. My friend isn't a pastor or youth worker. He's not on a church staff or on a leadership team. He doesn't spearhead a ministry area or make decisions about direction or spending or mission or vision. He's just a guy who works hard simply to get his young family to church most weeks.

Because he's my friend, he read a draft of this book. As a long-time church member who recently changed congregations with his family, his insight is this: in a church, it's really hard to see your own assumptions. You need new eyes to help you see what you take for granted.

In other words, the most natural thing in the world is to put together a group of leaders and influencers to evaluate if and how your congregation

---

[1] Peter Berger talks about how our mutually constructed understanding of reality is most stable when it is most taken for granted: "It is not enough that the individual look upon the key meanings of the social order as useful, desirable, or right. It is much better (better, that is, in terms of social stability) if he looks upon them as inevitable, as part and parcel of the universal 'nature of things'" *The Sacred Canopy*, Anchor Books (New York, 1969 and 1990), 24. That's one reason it is hard to notice, let alone change, "the way we do things around here."

might benefit from reevaluating your own discipleship defaults. But who would you put on that task force? Probably key staff people, important lay leaders, and other influencers in the congregation. Of course you need those people. But they are also the ones who are most enculturated into *the way we do things around here*. They are the ones most likely to assume *what we all take for granted*. They are fish well acclimated to their water.

If you really want to evaluate the default settings of your local congregational culture, you will want to include people who aren't as well connected and don't already know how things are just supposed to work. That's my friend's key insight.

So I hope you want to put together a team to think about what might shift in the life of your congregation if you moved from Assembly Line to Adventure, from Relay Race to Rope Team, or from Bank Vault to Banquet. But if you do, wonder what it would look like to include people who are new to your congregation, people on the fringe of your faith family, people on the way in (or even on the way out) of your fellowship.

Give them the floor and let them describe their experience. Ask them follow up questions about what seems natural and obvious to you. Get their help seeing the things that go without saying in your community.

But make sure to let them try on some different hats! They will probably harbor a natural fear of getting it wrong, so do everything you can to encourage a safe environment of experimentation where they can even talk like a heretic in order to help you understand their experience and see your own default settings.

We follow Jesus better when we follow him together. In this instance, a rope team mentality means that those who are least likely to be at the Center of influence[2] will have key insights into the way your community works.

It won't be easy to engage them. It might not be easy to hear what they have to say. But it just may be your best chance to actually notice your default settings. And **it's hard to change what you can't see.**

---

[2] The Center/Peripheral Image Schema we have noticed before means that those who are important, and who have power and influence, are naturally at the Center. We are less likely to assign weight or value to people on the margins, even when they are the ones who can see our community defaults most clearly because they have not been fully assimilated into our culture.

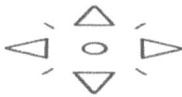

More to Rethink About

In Romans 12:2, the Apostle Paul writes: "Do not conform to the pattern of this world, but be transformed by the renewing of your mind" (NIV).

I think you could legitimately see default cultural values like efficiency and independence and standardization and an emphasis on personal achievement as part of the "pattern of this world." We don't *try* to adopt the most obvious and natural elements of our surrounding culture; we just *do*.

Paul's antidote to cultural assimilation is not more personal effort or better study habits. In fact, Paul's command in Romans 12 is formulated with a *passive* verb: "be transformed." That transformation is something that happens *to you* and has its origins *outside* of you. For Paul, that divine metamorphosis takes place by means of a mindset overhaul; a change of heart and understanding; a renewing of the way you think.

Once the Spirit begins this renewal process, it's hard to go back to the way things were. Like the guy who said he felt like he was on an assembly line during drive through communion, once you see the world through a new lens, you can't unsee it.

In many ways, this book has only scratched the surface, set your foot on a path of discovering the things we automatically take for granted. Some of those defaults can be both helpful and biblical. And some, as we have discovered, can get in the way of what we think they are helping us do.

If you have gotten all the way to the Conclusion of a book about noticing your defaults, then you have collected at least a few prevalent (and often problematic) metaphors the church tends to live by in this culture. Of course there are more. (There are so many more...)

If you begin with noticing the defaults in this book, you will start to shift what you think following Jesus looks like, and what feels obvious and natural to you. As you get into the habit of noticing those defaults, some other default settings may become obvious along the way.

I have started my own list. Maybe you can add to it as you go. If I ever write a sequel (or if you do), I would probably include some of these.

1) Windows or Waves? Something More than "Quiet Time"

We have a natural tendency to imagine the passing of time as a kind of movement (either you are moving toward the future or the future is moving toward you). The natural outcome of that way of experiencing the world is that you can "miss your window of opportunity." If you didn't read your Bible first thing in the morning, if you didn't share the Gospel when you had an opening, if you didn't say you are sorry when you had the chance, your thinking and emotions will tell you that the opportune time has passed. (And you missed it.)

I think following Jesus is much more like catching a wave of opportunity rather than hitting an ideal window: if that important moment of grace or engagement or blessing gets missed the first time, Jesus is faithful and will bring it back around. Wave thinking is more freeing and less achievement-driven than Window thinking when it comes to important moments of faith.

2) Spark or Spoke? Something More than "Gospel Motivation"

We tend to assume that complex problems have simple answers. When it comes to Christian living, we make it seem like believers will *just know* what to do and how to do it. We imagine the good news of the Gospel as a kind of spark, and once you light the fire, life transformation just happens naturally and automatically (of course, by the power of the Holy Spirit).

While I do believe life transformation is the work of the Spirit, I also believe human beings are complex creatures and human behavior is structured in ways that make some thinking, feeling, and acting seem obvious and natural while other habits seem onerous or impossible. So let the Spirit work; and also, create structures around faith-forming habits that enable a natural response.

The Spirit works through human means, and those means can support the work of the Spirit. Like a wheel needs spokes to provide the skeleton that enables movement, real people need personal, relational, and environmental factors to be aligned to spiritual growth. Very little growth in discipleship feels obvious or natural at the time, and providing the right support is essential.

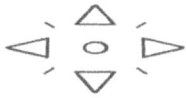

3) Red Ledger or Red Letter? Something More than "You Get What You Deserve"

One of the most damaging cultural defaults we live by is a sense that good things come to you because you are good; and if something bad happened, you probably deserved it. That cosmic karma approach not only leads to blaming other people for the situation they find themselves in, it also crushes even the most faithful Christians when tragedy strikes.

If my good life is evidence of God's pleasure, what do I think about God when the wheels fall off? There is a reason a majority of people in our country have an angry image of God.

That way of balancing a ledger sheet is living by the Law, and it permeates the air we breathe in our contemporary culture. The only hope of getting out from under the burden of that performance-driven paradigm, the only real comfort in times of tragedy, is to run back to the words of Jesus (Red Letters); his promises hold true regardless of our present circumstances.

4) Up and Out or Now and Not Yet? Something More than "Going to Heaven"

One final default setting to add to your list: Western Christianity tends to describe the goal of the Christian faith in terms of "dying and going to heaven." Trying to escape the (Bad) physical world by getting (Up) to the (Good) spiritual world is closer to Neo-Gnostic philosophy than it is to the hope of the New Testament.

Back in Chapter 3, we saw that salvation in the Bible comes *down* to us. We could add that salvation is also physical; it involves real, physical, resurrected bodies in a real, physical, New Creation.

Instead of framing our current existence as Down and salvation as Up and Out, the Bible places us on a timeline between the beginning of the End (the resurrection of Jesus) and the consummation of the End (his return in glory). Salvation is therefore portrayed as Already ours by faith, and Not Yet ours by sight. Inhabiting that dichotomy leads to very different ways of hoping, praying, thinking, feeling, living, and dying.

Those are my Top Four *Other* Ways Our Natural Defaults Misunderstand the Christian Faith. Maybe you'll be able to add to that bingo card as you go.

But *how* you add to that collection of defaults is really important. If any of these become one more item on a checklist, or one more law to uphold, or one more subject to grade on your Spiritual GPA, then we have fallen back into a performance-based religion that will slowly kill you even as it offers you more abundant life (if you only do this one more thing a little better...).

The bottom line is, you don't have to be any better at any of this to take a small next step following Jesus.

Even more importantly, **you don't have to be any better at any of this for Jesus to love you and to be proud of you and to want to walk with you.**

This book was never intended to give you more work to do. Just the opposite. This book is about leaning into what Jesus is up to, in ways that make following both more faithful and more fun.

Grant this, Lord, unto us all.

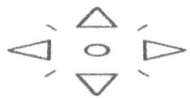

This Changes Everything

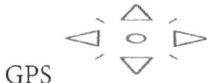

	GPA	GPS
Jesus	What a 4.0 looks like. The teacher who grades your work.	True North. The one who reveals to me where I am and points me in the right direction.
The Church	A classroom that teaches correct doctrine and moral behavior. Other students who are getting better grades than you.	A "walking with" community that looks for where Jesus is, and where Jesus is headed. People on the move.
The World	People who are getting worse grades than you, and aren't even taking the right classes!	A place to be explored; people to walk with, as you go.
The Goal	Get good grades (or at least better grades than some people I could mention). Keep your head down and graduate.	Be honest with where you are. Keep taking small next steps in the direction Jesus is leading. Invite others to walk with you.
My Role	Study hard. Do well on the tests. Don't speak out of turn. Be nice to other students. Be a role model for younger kids.	Notice where I am with Jesus. Drop my own judgment of where I am, and look for Jesus to lead me from here.
Key Thinking	Grading my performance tells me that I am doing better than some people and that I better work harder in the future.	Where am I right now? Where is Jesus? How does Jesus bring grace to where I am, and lead me from here?

Summary of the Conclusion

Making any kind of change will most naturally be experienced in terms of personal performance, individual effort, and success or failure. This GPA thinking can sneak into your thoughts and feelings even when you are trying to shift away from thinking and feeling that way. (I want to change my GPA mindset, but am I changing *enough* or should I be working harder to do better??) So take a deep breath, dial back the pressure, and look for how the Spirit is inviting you to take a small step forward. You can't change all of these defaults all at once; but that was never your job. Use these defaults as a kind of GPS that helps you see more clearly where you are, where Jesus is, and what the Spirit is shaping you into next. Don't make this all about getting it right. Do jump in and have fun.

• • •

For Further Reflection

Trying on an unusual hat while out shopping with friends is experimenting just for fun. What area of your faith walk could benefit from a little light-hearted experimentation? Come up with three intriguing things to try. Try one of them and share how it went.

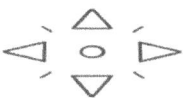

(1) Assembly Line or Adventure; (2) High Bar or Clay Jar; (3) Relay Race or Rope Team; (4) Bank Vault or Banquet; (5) Pitched Battle or Pitched Tent: Which of the five main defaults in this book seemed most significant to you? Describe how you see that default at work and a few experiments you could run to bring in a new perspective.

Do you generally default back to GPA thinking, or is GPS your home base? How can you tell?

If you gave this book to a friend, what would you want to tell them about it?

If you had the knowledge, skill, time, and desire to write a book about one of the topics suggested in the More to Rethink About section, which one would it be? (1) Something More than "Quiet Time"; (2) Something More than "Gospel Motivation"; (3) Something More than "You Get What You Deserve"; or (4) Something More than "Going to Heaven"? Why that one?

Has this book affected to any degree how you think, how you talk, how you read the Bible, or how you pray? In what ways?

Acknowledgments

The metaphors we use to frame the experience of writing a book are numerous: Constructing a Building, Giving Birth, Taming a Wild Beast, Defeating a Wrestling Opponent, Raising a Child, Cooking a Soup, and Going on a Journey, to name a few. And so, I have had many architects, master builders, cheerleaders, coaches, taste-testers, and traveling companions along the way. It takes a village.

My dear friend, Conrad Gempf, has had his fingers in the pot from the very beginning. Some of my favorite paragraphs owe much to his architectural skill, and you have been spared some of my worst writing due to his friendly critique and expert scalpel. His steadfast faith in this book has been a sustaining boon.

My cousin and friend, Ken Miller, has been part of the ongoing discussion about language and metaphor along the way as long as I can remember. His coaching on all things entrepreneurial has been invaluable, and his dogged support has gotten me through more than one difficult stretch of the road.

Ted Hopkins became a close friend and my pastor in the midst of this journey, and his careful work with Church and Culture helped shape the later chapters, for which I am grateful.

My best friend from Seminary, Steve Wiechman, has lived this book over years of ministry with me, given me faithful feedback, and even failed at test-driving some of these chapters in ways that helped us move forward, anyway.

Multiple congregations have experimented with the contents of different chapters at different times, and I am thankful for their partnership. Among many are Peace in Hurst, TX; St. Luke and St. Paul in Ann Arbor, MI; St. Paul in Harlingen, TX; and Shepherd of the Lakes in Brighton, MI.

Brett Jordan's graphic design work with the cover and (my niece) Lucie Orozco's chapter headings added depth and fragrance to the soup I would not want to do without. The best meals are shared with friends and family.

My Great Uncle, Professor "Rev." Francis Rossow (in his 100th year on this planet), my Mom (Deanna), and my Uncle Steve shared their proofreading prowess. In so many ways, this book has been a family affair, so thank you to my wife Miriam and my children, Naomi, Liz, Kate, and Caleb. Your loving support is more powerful than you know. And to my Older Brother, I would say thank you, and we love you, and come back soon; we miss you.

Works Cited

Theology and Discipleship

Darrell L. Guder, ed. *Missional Church: A Vision for the Sending of the Church in North America.* Eerdmans, 1998.

Theodore J. Hopkins. *Christ, Church, and World: Bonhoeffer and Lutheran Ecclesiology after Christendom.* Fortress Academic, 2021.

Francis Rossow. *Preaching the Creative Gospel Creatively.* Concordia Publishing House, 1983.

Justin Rossow. *Delight! Discipleship as the Adventure of Loving and Being Loved.* Next Step Press, 2020.

Leopoldo A. Sánchez M. *Sculptor Spirit: Models of Sanctification from Spirit Christology.* IVP Academic, 2019.

Samuel Wells. *A Nazareth Manifesto: Being with God.* Wiley Blackwell, 2015.

Culture

Peter L. Berger. *The Sacred Canopy: Elements of a Sociological Theory of Religion.* Anchor Books, 1969, 1990. Hardcover originally published by Doubleday, 1967.

CGP Grey. "This Video Will Make You Angry." *YouTube.* Available at: https://youtu.be/rE3j_RHkqJc.

Gregory Smith and Alan Cooperman. "Has the rise of religious 'nones' come to an end in the U.S.?" Pew Research Center, January 2024. Available at https://www.pewresearch.org/short-reads/2024/01/24/has-the-rise-of-religious-nones-come-to-an-end-in-the-us/.

Ed Stetzer. *Christians in the Age of Outrage: How to Bring Our Best When the World is at its Worst.* Tyndale Momentum, 2018.

David Foster Wallace. "This is Water." Commencement speech at Kenyon College, 2005. Available at http://bulletin-archive.kenyon.edu/x4280.html.

Metaphor Theory

Jerome Feldman. *From Molecule to Metaphor: A Neural Theory of Language.* MIT Press, 2008.

Raymond Gibbs and Teenie Matlock. "Metaphor, Imagination, and Simulation: Psycholinguistic Evidence." In Gibbs, ed., *The Cambridge Handbook of Metaphor and Thought.* Cambridge University Press, 2008 (161–176).

Bonnie Howe. *Because You Bear This Name: Conceptual Metaphor and the Moral Meaning of 1 Peter.* Brill, 2006.

Mark Johnson. *The Body in the Mind: The Bodily Basis of Meaning, Imagination, and Reason.* University of Chicago Press, 1987.

Zoltán Kövecses. *Metaphor: A Practical Introduction.* Oxford University Press, 2002.

———. *Metaphor in Culture: Universality and Variation.* Cambridge University Press, 2006.

George Lakoff. "The Contemporary Theory of Metaphor." In A. Ortony, ed., *Metaphor and Thought.* 2nd ed. Cambridge University Press, 1993 (202-251).

———. "The Neural Theory of Metaphor." In Raymond Gibbs, ed., *The Cambridge Handbook of Metaphor and Thought.* Cambridge University Press, 2008 (17-38).

———. *Women, Fire, and Dangerous Things: What Categories Reveal about the Mind.* University of Chicago Press, 1987.

George Lakoff and Mark Johnson. *Metaphors We Live By.* University of Chicago Press, 1981. Reprint ed., 2003.

———. *Philosophy in the Flesh: The Embodied Mind and Its Challenge to Western Thought.* Basic Books, 1999.

George Lakoff and Mark Turner. *More than Cool Reason: A Field Guide to Poetic Metaphor.* University of Chicago Press, 1989.

Carolyn Parkinson, Shari Liu, and Thalia Wheatley. "A Common Cortical Metric for Spatial, Temporal, and Social Distance." *The Journal of Neuroscience*, January 29, 2014, 34 (5):1979–1987.

Justin Rossow. *Preaching Metaphor: How to Shape Sermons that Shape People.* Next Step Press, 2019.

———. "Preaching the Story Behind the Image: A Narrative Approach to Metaphor for Preaching." PhD Diss. Concordia Seminary—St. Louis, 2009.

———. "Shaping Sermons that Shape People." In Allen Nauss, ed., *The Pastor's Brain Manual: A Fascinating Work in Progress.* Lutheran University Press, 104-131.

Paul Thibodeau and Lera Boroditsky. "Metaphors We Think With: The Role of Metaphor in Reasoning." PLoS ONE 6(2): e16782. February, 2011. Available at: https://doi.org/10.1371/journal.pone.0016782.

Mark Turner. *The Literary Mind: The Origins of Thought and Language.* Oxford University Press, 1996.

Richard M. White. *The Structure of Metaphor: The Way the Language of Metaphor Works.* Blackwell Publishers, 1996.

Index of Metaphors

Adventure, see Faith is a Journey

Argument is Dance, 146-149, 151, 158, 160

Argument is War, 6, 37, 138-143, 147-148, 151-152, 155, 157

Assembly Line, see Discipling is Mass Production

Banquet, see The Kingdom of God is a Banquet

Bootstrapping, 44, 49, 51, 62 n. 11

Boundary Issues, see The Container Schema

Central is Important, 113 n. 6, 119, 130-131, 170 n. 2

Change Your Filter/Lens, see Knowing is Seeing

The Container Schema, 109-112
    The Believer is a Container, 128-130, 159
    Boundary Issues are the Boundary of a Container, 97, 113-118, 141, 157
    A Faith Community (Church) is a Container, 122-115, 130 n. 14
    Jesus is a Container, 130 n.14
    A Nation is a Container, 141
    People are Objects in a Container, 115
    A Social Group is a Container, see A Faith Community is a Container
    Your Heart is a Container, 113
    Your Brain is a Container, 113

The Church
    The Church is a Container, see the Container Schema
    The Church is a Centered Set, 122 n. 10
    The Church is a Factory, 17
    The Church is a Flock, 121-123
    The Church is a Portable Temple/Tent, 154, 159

Crime
    Crime is a Virus, 33-35
    Crime is a Wild Beast, 33-35

Dependence is Down, 59-63

Discipleship
    Discipleship is Apprenticeship, 30
    Discipleship is Being Shaped, see Potter and Clay
    Discipleship is Whitewater Kayaking, see Life is a Journey
    Discipling is Mass Production/Producing an End Product, 14-19, 100-101
    Discipling is Walking With, see Life is a Journey

Embodied Simulation, 71 n. 1

Faith
    Faith is a Journey, see Life is a Journey
    Faith is a Physical Object, 78; see also Passing on the Faith
    Faith is a Plant, 95
    Faith is a Relay Race, see Passing on the Faith
    Faith is Spiritual Warfare, 145-146
    Faith is Walking the Emmaus Road, see Life is a Journey

God's Word
    God's Word is a Lamp, 94 n. 2
    God's Word is Seed, see Faith is a Plant

Good is Up, 45-55, 59, 64, 166, 173
    Active is Up, 47, 51-52, 55, 59-60, 62, 64
    Authority is Up, 46, 64
    Conscious is Up, 46
    Control is Up, 46-47, 51-52, 55, 57, 59-60, 62, 64
    Happy is Up, 46-47
    More is Up, 47, 49, 50 n.4, 51-54, 57, 59-60, 62, 64

GPA, see Life is a Competition

GPS, see Life is a Journey

The Holy Spirit is Fire, 98 n. 4

Image Schemas
    The Center/Peripheral Image Schema, see Central is Important
    The In/Out Image Schema, see The Container Schema

Jesus
- Jesus is a Container, see the Container Schema
- Jesus is the Door, 120-121
- Jesus is an Example, 49-52, 54, 59-61
- Jesus is the Gate, 119-121
- Jesus is the Good Shepherd, 119, 121, 123
- Jesus is Inside the Believer, see the Container Schema
- Jesus is the Assembly Line Foreman, 15, 28
- Jesus is a Sculptor's Model, 56
- Jesus is the Tent/Tabernacle, 154, 160
- Jesus is a Treasure, 128, 130, 130 n. 14
- Jesus is the Vine, 61-62
- Jesus is the Way, 120-121

The Kingdom of God is a Banquet, 36, 124-132

Knowing is Seeing
- Change of Thinking is Change of Seeing (Filter, Lens), 39-41, 96-104, 148
- Rethinking is Reframing, 36-38, 89-104
- What We Don't Think About is Invisible, 31-32, 90, 169-170
- See also Snapshot and Collage

Life is a Competition
- Evaluating Your Life is Grading on a Scale, 47-48, 51-52, 166-167, 174
- Goals in Life are a High Bar, 45, 47-48, 49-51
- Life is a Race, 94; see also Passing on the Faith

Life is a Journey, 79 n. 6, 81 n. 7
- Discipleship is Whitewater Kayaking, 56 n. 7
- Discipleship is Walking With, 21-24, 100-101
- Evaluating Your Faith is Checking a GPS, 167-168
- Faith is an Adventure, 20-21, 26
- Faith is Mountaineering on a Rope Team, 78-85, 93-95, 100-101
- Faith is Walking the Emmaus Road, 20 n. 3

Moral Accounting, 173

Orientational Metaphors, 46 n. 1, 47, 59, 62; see also Spatialization Metaphors

Passing on the Faith, 71-78, 79 n. 6, 82-83, 85, 91-95, 100

People are Animals
    The Parable of the Fishing Net, 118 n. 8, 124 n.11
    People are Fish (and Assumptions are Water), 31-36, 39-41, 113, 117, 170
    People are Sheep, 145; see the Church is a Flock, Jesus is the Good Shepherd
    People are Wolves, 45
    The Sheep and the Goats, 118 n. 8, 124 n.11

People are Objects
    People are Musical Instruments (and Disagreement is Dissonance), 150-151
    New People are Raw Materials, see Discipling is Mass Production
    People are Objects in a Container, see The Container Schema

People are Plants
    Believers are Branches, see Jesus is the Vine
    Having Faith or Good Works is Bearing Fruit, 62-63, 95
    The Parable of the Wheat and Tares, 118 n. 8, 124 n.11, 131
    People Ready to Hear are Fields Ripe for Harvest, 98, 149
    People are Peas/Beans (and Inter-personal Tension is a Trellis), 149-152

Potter and Clay, 56-59, 59 n. 9, 54

Relational Distance is Physical Distance, 72 n. 2, 118 n. 7

Relay Race, see Passing on the Faith

Salvation is Down, 53-56

Snapshot and Collage, 94-95, 103, 145-146, 152, 155

Spatialization Metaphors, 46-47, 48-49, 62, 79 n. 6; see Orientational Metaphors

Time is Movement, 172

Trying Something New is Running an Experiment, 25, 83, 131, 149, 170, 176

Up/Down Image Schema, see Good is Up

Vine and Branches, see Jesus is the Vine

Warfare, see Argument is War

Scripture Index

Genesis
  2, 153
  3, 153
  11, 153
  11:3-5, 54
  12, 153
  12:1, 167
  18, 128

Exodus
  3:8, 53
  19:11, 53

Deuteronomy
  6:7, 84
  10:19, 144

2 Kings
  2, 94

The Psalms, 144

Proverbs
  26:4-5, 102

Isaiah
  64:1, 53

Joel
  144 n. 5

Matthew
  3, 55
  4, 55
  5-7, 145
  8:20, 129 n. 13
  10, 145
  10:40, 129
  13:24-30, 118 n. 8
  13:47-50, 118 n. 8
  25:1-13, 118 n. 8
  25:14-30, 118 n. 8
  25:31-46, 118 n. 8
  25:40, 128
  26:73, 126
  28:19, 14

Mark
  1, 58
  4:25-27, 95

Luke
  2, 145
  4, 55
  9, 98 n. 3
  9:58, 129 n. 13
  14, 124
  14:23, 124
  10, 127, 145
  19:5, 127
  19:9, 127
  24, 20 n. 3

John
- 1:14, 153
- 4, 96, 98, 99, 149, 151
- 4:7-8, 96
- 4:31-33, 97
- 4:33-35, 98
- 4:42, 99
- 6:33, 53
- 10:9, 119
- 10:14, 121

- 13-15, 62
- 13, 50, 61
- 13:12-15, 54
- 13:15, 49, 59
- 13:20, 60, 128
- 13:34, 59
- 13:34-35, 54

- 14, 61
- 14:6, 120
- 14:10-11, 60
- 14:12, 49, 60
- 14:16-18, 61
- 14:20, 61
- 14:23, 61

- 15, 61
- 15:4, 62
- 15:5, 95
- 15:9-11, 62
- 19, 128

Acts
- 2, 55
- 8, 98 n. 4

Romans
- 1:11-12, 95
- 6, 55
- 12:2, 171

1 Corinthians
- 3:6, 95

2 Corinthians
- 4:7, 130 n. 14

Galatians
- 1, 145

Ephesians
- 2, 56, 145, 154
- 6, 145

Philippians
- 2:12-13, 56 n. 7, 62
- 3, 145
- 3:19-20, 53

1 Thessalonians
- 4:16, 53

2 Timothy
- 4:7, 94

Revelation
- 7, 21
- 19:9, 124
- 21:3, 153
- 21:10, 53

For bonus material, don't forget to visit the

Escaping the Assembly Line Resource Page

https://bit.ly/etal-Resource

More from Next Step Press

Delight! Discipleship as the Adventure of Loving and Being Loved by Justin Rossow received the 2020 BIBA® Award for best independently published book in the Christian category. It explores God's great joy in you, and how God intends the feeling to be mutual. Don't miss this breath of fresh air for your faith! More at **https://bit.ly/NSP-Delight**.

Today Is Where the Gift Is continues the Tales from the Next Step Community series. As a collection of blogs and articles from over a dozen different authors, and edited by Justin Rossow, this volume is a finalist in the 2025 Christian Indie Awards in the Anthology category. Inside you'll find real help from real people who are just trying to take a small next step. See **https://bit.ly/TNSC-4**.

The *My Next Step* Series is designed to equip your next step, following Jesus. A great tool for individuals, small groups, and congregations. The three volumes together help you cultivate a discipling culture: **https://bit.ly/Next-Step-Trilogy**.

Find the entire Next Step Press library at **https://bit.ly/NSP-books**.

www.ingramcontent.com/pod-product-compliance
Lightning Source LLC
Chambersburg PA
CBHW062214080426
42734CB00010B/1891